IMAGES OF SPORT

RUGBY LEAGUE
IN MANCHESTER

IMAGES OF SPORT

RUGBY LEAGUE IN MANCHESTER

GRAHAM MORRIS

TEMPUS

Front cover: Australia attack the Belle Vue Rangers defensive line during the second match of their 1948 tour of Great Britain at Belle Vue Stadium, the speedway referees' box above the stand providing the backdrop at the famous Hyde Road raceway.

Frontispiece: Bob Wilson, the charismatic Broughton Rangers captain who led his team to glory in the opening decade of the twentieth century. Under his command, the Rangers won both the Championship and Challenge Cup in 1901/02 – the first ever 'Rugby League' double – and the Lancashire Cup of 1906. In addition to playing 256 times for Broughton Rangers, he made 16 appearances for Lancashire – who he also skippered – and represented England against Other Nationalities in January 1905 at Bradford. The Rangers enjoyed substantial support from amongst the local Jewish population and it was said that Wilson (who was not Jewish himself): 'Had a good following from the Jewish community who had great faith in him, shouting "Give the ball to Wilson!"'

First published 2003

Tempus Publishing Limited
The Mill, Brimscombe Port,
Stroud, Gloucestershire, GL5 2QG
www.tempus-publishing.com

British Library Cataloguing in Publication Data.
A catalogue record for this book is available from the British Library.

ISBN 0 7524 3087 4

Typesetting and origination by Tempus Publishing Limited.
Printed in Great Britain by Midway Colour Print, Wiltshire.

Contents

Acknowledgements

There are many people, to whom I am indebted for their enthusiastic support whilst compiling this book, but, in particular, I must mention John Edwards and Eric Shorrock. John shares my fascination in what was, until now, the forgotten history of Broughton (later Belle Vue) Rangers and his earlier research and collection of newspaper cuttings and photographs of the club has greatly enhanced my own. Eric, a former supporter from the Rangers days at Belle Vue has, both graciously and patiently, put his memorabilia and wonderful store of memories at my disposal.

Others, who have my unstinting thanks for helping me to collect, over many years, items and information relevant to the sport in the Manchester region, are: Jack Arrowsmith, Frank Bailey, Tony Collins, Trevor Delaney, Richard Dalglish, Robert Gate, Graham Gerrard, Jeffrey and Marcel Glaskie, Michael Hall, John Hampton, Andrew Hardcastle, Simon Ingles, John Jenkins, John M. Jones, Michael Latham, Keith Nutter, Ron Robinson, Gladys Smith and John Riding. I also acknowledge the excellent work of Irvin Saxton and the Rugby League Record Keepers Club.

I am very grateful for the help I received from the Lancashire County Rugby Football Union, the respective staff at Manchester Central Library, Salford Local History Library (Tim Ashworth, Sandra Hayton and Trish Nuttall) and Manchester Southern Cemetery records office (Paul Clarke) during my research. I would also like to record my appreciation of *The Independent* (Dave Hadfield in particular), the *Daily Telegraph*, Lancashire Publications Limited, League Publications Limited (Tim Butcher) and the *Manchester Evening News* for kindly allowing me to reproduce certain items.

Billy Stott (left), the former Broughton Rangers captain, receives a special award, presented by sports journalist Jimmy Breen, at Belle Vue Stadium on 31 August 1946. It commemorated his match-winning performance at Wembley the previous May, in which he kicked a difficult last-minute penalty to win the Challenge Cup for his club, Wakefield Trinity, over Wigan. The actual ball used in the final – autographed by the players of both teams – was mounted on a plinth that included the inscription: 'Presented to Billy Stott, the hero of the match, by his colleagues at Belle Vue Gardens, Manchester.'

Introduction

Whenever I become involved in polite conversation on visits overseas and answer 'Manchester' in response to the standard 'Where are you from?' question, the usual retort is 'Ah, Manchester United!' I am sure it is an experience shared by most Mancunians on their travels, such is the worldwide fame of the team from Old Trafford. Together with the huge support enjoyed by derby rivals Manchester City, it adds up to the region being one of the hottest spots in English soccer.

As popular as it undoubtedly is, however, the sporting heritage of Manchester goes far beyond the boundaries of Association Football. In the mid-1990s, it was reported the area boasted a staggering 12,000 sporting organisations catering for 300,000 competitors – the highest in the United Kingdom outside of London. The decision to host the seventeenth Commonwealth Games at the new City of Manchester Stadium during July and August 2002 could not have been more appropriate.

English Heritage also chose the city to unveil an initiative aimed at recognising the nation's sporting legacy and the historical importance of its surviving venues. Manchester (which they quoted as 'the sporting capital of the north') and the surrounding districts was considered the ideal location to carry out the initial study. The official launch day at the Manchester Conference Centre in June 2002 covered a variety of sports, one of which was Rugby League, with archive film featuring the Belle Vue Rangers and Salford clubs shown to attendees.

Long before United and City dominated the Manchester sporting scene, football played under the 'rugby' code of rules held sway. Indeed, when the Lancashire County Rugby Union was founded at the Albion Hotel, Manchester, in December 1881, the region had strong representation including Broughton, Broughton Rangers, Cheetham, Free Wanderers (based in Fallowfield), Manchester (Whalley Range), Manchester Athletic (Alexandra Park), Manchester Rangers (Old Trafford), Salford and Swinton.

The link with rugby is forged stronger when it is realised that William Webb Ellis – for years credited as the founder of the handling game – was Christened in Salford during 1807 and probably born in Manchester. Although modern sports historians believe the legend surrounding Ellis who, it is claimed, 'first took the ball and ran with it' during a match at Rugby School in 1823, to be untrue, that account is perpetuated with the naming of the Rugby Union World Cup in his honour. The birthplace of the legendary Ellis remained a mystery for years, until Richard Dalglish, whilst undertaking research for his 1982 book *Red, Black & Blue* (the history of Liverpool Rugby Union Club), painstakingly attempted to unravel the mystery. The evidence supporting Manchester and Salford's claim is included in the opening chapter of this compilation.

Of those clubs named above, only Manchester – founded in 1860 – remain as a Rugby Union outfit. Interestingly, Cheshire-based neighbours Sale, who began life a year later, share their longevity, with just Liverpool (in 1857 and merged as Liverpool-St Helens since 1986) and Blackheath (1858) claiming greater age amongst current English clubs.

The only other survivors amongst our list of pioneering clubs are Salford and Swinton who, along with Broughton Rangers, defected to the Northern Union (known as the Rugby Football League from 1922) during the mid-1890s. Strictly speaking, all three come under the auspices of Manchester's twin city of Salford although – to the chagrin of every proud Salfordian and Swintonian alike – they are often touted as being Manchester clubs, all being within a relatively short distance from Manchester city centre. In fact, when Salford and Swinton met in the 1900 Challenge

Cup final, they were hailed as 'the best two supported teams in Manchester' and they themselves encouraged the misnomer when combining as a 'Manchester XIII' to oppose the 1961 New Zealand touring side. Curiously, the birthplace of the Salford City Reds (as they are now called) was in Manchester, founded by the boys of Cavendish Street School, Hulme, during 1873.

Broughton Rangers, whose famous old grounds at Wheater's Field and The Cliff were just a half-mile from the Manchester/Salford border, eventually became Manchester's very own Rugby League club when it transferred operations to the Belle Vue Speedway Stadium, Gorton, during 1933. Renamed Belle Vue Rangers from 1946, it is the only senior Rugby League club, to date, to have had a base within the Manchester boundary.

Over the years, Manchester has hosted many major Rugby League occasions at venues such as Fallowfield Stadium, Manchester City's Maine Road enclosure, the White City Stadium and Manchester United's renowned Old Trafford. These were mostly high-profile clashes, attracting some of Rugby League's biggest crowds to witness occasions such as Challenge Cup, Championship and Premiership finals and, in recent years, Super League Grand Finals and Test Matches. A bid by Rugby League's hierarchy to stage a Great Britain-Australia Test Match at the new City of Manchester Stadium during November 2003 has been thwarted, officials of Manchester City AFC understandably concerned about damage to the pitch at the start of their inaugural 2003/04 season there. It is, however, surely a matter of time before that magnificent venue joins Manchester's list of thirteen-a-side settings.

In the pages that follow, we recall those great games and take a look at the contribution of the area's three professional Rugby League clubs: Broughton (later Belle Vue) Rangers, Salford and Swinton. The life and times of the latter two, and the achievements of the famous players that graced these great clubs, are related in detail in separate *Images of Sport* titles from Tempus. In this edition, I have placed the emphasis on recalling some of the major events hosted at their famous enclosures. Salford's home at The Willows was – particularly in the earlier years of the twentieth century – the choice for many major finals, including decisive matches for the Championship, Challenge Cup and Lancashire Cup. Swinton's Station Road ground can claim to have seen more big occasions than any other in the Manchester area, with a list covering 19 internationals and 26 finals across various competitions.

The Rangers, one of the most famous clubs in the sport's history, were – in season 1901/02 – the first to achieve a Rugby League 'double' of Championship and Challenge Cup. In this volume, we take the opportunity to chronicle their proud story – being the first book ever to do so – using many photographs and images not previously published. Collecting illustrative material for the Rangers was particularly challenging as few archive items survive, due in the main to two unfortunate incidents. Firstly, a fire damaged the club pavilion at The Cliff in 1931, destroying approximately thirty historic photographs, and further treasures were lost when the Lake Hotel headquarters on Hyde Road (used following the move to Belle Vue in 1933) was demolished in the 1980s, many items finding their way into a waste skip – although, fortunately, some were recovered. I am particularly grateful, therefore, to the many people who enthusiastically answered my appeals in the press, unearthing many pictures and generally increasing my memorabilia of the club. Those that came to my rescue and provided their valued assistance receive due and appreciative recognition under the 'Acknowledgements' section of this book. One consequence of those mishaps has been the difficulty in identifying individuals on the earliest team groups that remain, although an attempt has been made to provide the reader with as much information as possible and, hopefully, this does not detract too much from your enjoyment. Please read on and enjoy the fascinating story of Rugby League in Manchester.

Graham Morris
October 2003

one

Early Years in Manchester

In the formative years of football during the 1860s, '70s, and '80s, it was the oval ball of the rugby code that dominated in Manchester. The massive influence of soccer on the city's sporting culture was still some way into the future. The creation of the (Association) Football League in 1888, although having strong North West representation amongst its inaugural twelve clubs, was bereft of Manchester connections other than that the key foundation meeting took place at the former Royal Hotel in Piccadilly. The involvement of Ardwick (the future Manchester City) and Newton Heath (Manchester United) in the competition did not come about until 1892.

The Manchester (Rugby) Football Club – still flourishing in Cheadle Hulme – was particularly dominant during this early period. The fact that they took the title of Manchester Football Club as early as 1860 illustrates how far ahead rugby was in the vicinity, leaving their soccer cousins, years later, to add 'City' (in 1894) and 'United' (1902) when adopting the city name. The Manchester club's former Whalley Range enclosure was home to the county team for many years and England played seven internationals there between 1880 and 1892.

As the twentieth century dawned, the rising popularity of soccer had edged rugby from the limelight – not just in Manchester, but throughout the country, a position held to this day. The Rugby Football Union itself was culpable in this situation arising. Whereas soccer legalised professionalism in 1885, paving the way for competitive leagues and increased spectator interest, the RFU refused to contemplate such a step until 1995, holding back from recognising league competitions until the first 'official' championship commenced in 1987, fearing it would encourage player payments.

Those concerns were not without justification. In 1892, the Lancashire Rugby Union Committee reluctantly sanctioned the Lancashire Club Championship. Leading 'working class' clubs Broughton Rangers, Salford (the first winners) and Swinton eagerly joined, whilst the Manchester club – a more 'elite' organisation whose players had been through public schools and universities – felt such a contest was not in the sporting spirit. Accusations of illicit payments soon surfaced, Salford being one of several 'guilty' clubs suspended in 1894/95. Broughton Rangers hit the headlines when they tempted Welsh international halves, the brothers David and Evan James, to Manchester in October 1892, the pair subsequently being suspended as 'professionals'.

The reluctance of the Rugby Union authorities to permit payments played a major part in the infamous split of 1895 ('The Great Schism') when most of the leading northern clubs broke away to form the Northern Union (renamed 'The Rugby Football League' in 1922). This mass defection diluted the potency of England's national side for years and cost Rugby Union huge areas of patronage in the North, as many of the lost clubs enjoyed massive support in the towns and communities they represented.

THE

Register of Trinity Church Salford
Christenings 1807 *Burials 1807*

The name of William Webb Ellis is the first Christenings entry on the register of (Sacred) Trinity Church Salford for January 1807. It confirms Ellis was born several weeks previously on 24 November 1806 to James (Ellis) and Ann (Ellis, nee Webb). Although his exact place of birth is not given, Webb Ellis himself later entered 'Manchester' as his birthplace in a census return. Sacred Trinity Church, which still exists today, is 100 yards from the Manchester-Salford border. A stone plaque (placed in the grounds of Rugby School in 1900) famously claims that Ellis 'with a fine disregard for the rules of football as played in his time first took the ball in his arms and ran with it thus originating the distinctive feature of the rugby game'. That inscription is based on the reminiscences of Matthew Bloxam, a pupil at Rugby School during the period in question, who wrote in 1880 that Webb Ellis had carried out his deed in 1823.

Robert ('Bob') L. Seddon was one of the original members of the Broughton Rangers club which was founded in 1877 as Broughton, adding the 'Rangers' tag for the 1878/79 campaign, their second season. Playing initially amongst the backs, he graduated to the forwards cementing his reputation as the 'Broughton Steam Engine'. For three seasons (from 1881/82) he played for rivals Broughton, returning to the Rangers for 1884/85. Accused of professionalism by members of his own club (relating to a dispute over a payment claim of £2 for a dress suit!) but found 'not guilty' by the Lancashire RU committee, he left the Rangers in October 1887 and looked set to rejoin Broughton before settling for Swinton. He represented England 3 times, the North of England (in the prestigious annual fixture against the South) on 4 occasions, and appeared in 17 matches (11 whilst with the Rangers) for Lancashire. In 1888, he had the honour of leading the first British rugby party to the Antipodes, tragically drowning in a boating accident in Australia midway through the tour. A memorial was erected near the scene in Maitland, New South Wales. He is seen here in his 1888 red-white-and-blue-hooped tour jersey.

Roger Walker was a major influence on the early history of the Manchester (Rugby) Football Club and, indeed, the sport in general. An outstanding forward he was reputed to be 'the greatest hacker of all time', one account saying he 'would gather the ball in his own half and hack his way through the entire opposition to score' (this description presumably relates to kicking/dribbling the ball, the term 'hacking' normally meant kicking the shins of an opponent who had the ball). He captained Manchester for seven seasons, and was later club president. He also represented England 5 times (1874 to 1880) and played for the North of England on 6 occasions. Walker was president of the Rugby Football Union from 1894 to 1896 and a member of the International Board from 1895 to 1899. He also managed the British Rugby Union team that toured South Africa in 1896.

Jim Valentine is regarded as the most legendary name in the proud history of the Swinton club, joining them in 1883. In addition to being chosen as captain of the team, the brilliant centre also led the Lancashire side regularly during his phenomenal 56 county outings (the official Lancashire RU centenary brochure states 60, although this is probably based on 'selected' teams in the county minutes). He played for England 4 times (1890 to 1896) and made 7 appearances for the North of England. When Swinton joined the Northern Union in 1896, he earned further glory under the auspices of the new code, adding 5 more county caps and – his greatest triumph – leading Swinton to victory in the 1900 Challenge Cup final against Salford. Tragically, Valentine was killed by lightening in 1904, just three years after his final senior match for Swinton. Both of the photographs reproduced on this page appeared in a series of 224 'Famous Footballers', published in 1895.

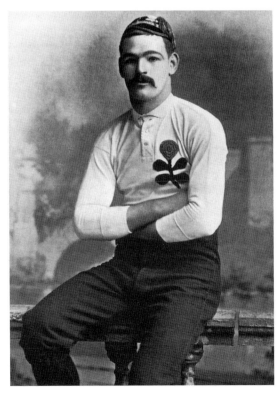

Harry Eagles – depicted here in a drawing that appeared in the sports paper *Black and White* during October 1887 – was the most revered of all Salford players during the club's early years in the Rugby Union fold. He joined Salford in 1881 and continued to wear their colours until 1892, being captain in 1888/89 and 1890/91, later joining the committee. An industrious forward, he was the first Salford player to gain international recognition through his selection for England in 1888. Due to England being embroiled in a dispute with the three other home unions at the time, he never actually played, although he did receive his 'cap'. His consolation came later in the year when he was included in the first British side to tour Australia and New Zealand, amazingly appearing in all 52 matches. His also represented Lancashire 18 times and the North of England on 3 occasions.

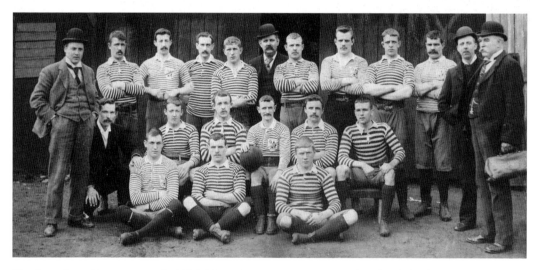

The Broughton Rangers team in 1886. There is no surviving caption but the club's five Lancashire county players of the time can be identified through their 'red rose' badges. Bob Seddon is standing, third from left, with Johnny Robertson seated centre (with ball). The remaining three (standing, fifth and third from right, and on the ground, left) will be Sam Simpson, Arthur Teggin and Jack Tune – although, unfortunately, it is not possible to determine which is which. Robertson became captain during 1882/83, retaining the role a further six seasons until his retirement. The club began life on a field at Walness (a site that is now the David Lewis Recreation Ground), near Peel Park, in 1877. Situated by Walness Bridge on the banks of the River Irwell, the playing area often flooded through the rising waters of the Irwell. It was during their tenure at Walness that the Rangers had Seddon, Teggin (like Seddon a founding player at the club) and Arthur 'Artie' Royle capped for England.

The Broughton (Rugby) Football Club was founded in 1869 as Broughton Wasps by pupils of Broughton College, establishing their home at Cliff Point in Higher Broughton (close to Broughton Rangers' future home at The Cliff). In 1878, they amalgamated with local club Wellington, changing their name to Broughton, a move that forced the existing Walness-based Broughton club, formed the previous year, to adopt the title of Broughton Rangers. Broughton – credited with introducing 'the passing game' into Lancashire rugby – were, along with Manchester, a 'gentlemen's' club, exemplified by John Henry Payne (originally a Wellington player), their most capped England player with 7 appearances from 1882 to 1885, who had played for Cambridge University. In addition to Payne, F. Moss (3 times) and CM Sawyer (2) were also chosen for England.

Broughton's headquarters was at the Griffin Hotel, situated on Lower Broughton Road, giving rise to their famous nickname of 'The Griffins' (note the players' badges in the team group above). On 29 October 1878, they staged what is reputed to be the first ever floodlit rugby match in Britain (fifteen days after the first 'floodlit' soccer match in Sheffield). A reported 8,000 to 9,000 curious spectators watched as 'A.T. Bowman's Team' (effectively Broughton) defeated 'W. Longshaw's Team' (Swinton) under 'Gramme's Light', which consisted of two lights in opposite corners mounted on 30-foot poles. Broughton were one of the few 'elite' clubs (the rest being considered 'working class') to join the new Lancashire Club Championship in 1892/93. They performed badly and, relegated to the Second Division for 1894/95, withdrew in mid-season, reasoning they were 'trying to raise the social tone of the club', implying that competitive rugby was not the 'done thing'.

The loss of so many crowd-pulling senior clubs to the Northern Union in the mid-1890s saw attendances dwindle, leading to an adverse bank balance, the club disbanding after the 1897/98 season. One journalist lamented they were 'the once-honoured and once-feared Griffins of Broughton Cliff'. Their Cliff Point ground was taken over by Broughton Park RUFC (founded in 1882), who today play in Chorlton-cum-Hardy. Although the names in the photograph are not known, this historic picture almost certainly dates from the late-1880s.

Harry Chapman – seen here in his Lancashire county cap and jersey – joined the Rangers from Broughton Hornets as an eighteen-year-old in September 1890. Broughton-born, he was in the Rangers team for the club's first Northern Union fixture – following their withdrawal from the Rugby Union – on 7 September 1895, a 9–0 home defeat by Wigan. Elected captain in 1896, he proved an influential figure in winning the Lancashire Championship of 1896/97 and 1898/99, the first honours secured by the club. Noted as an elusive and skilful centre and 'an amazingly clever drop-kicker', his Rangers playing career embraced 11 seasons, including 122 appearances under Northern Union rules. He also made 7 appearances for Lancashire under the latter regime. Chapman missed the whole of the 1899/1900 campaign due to a pre-season practice game injury and was unable to reproduce his form after he came back, his final outing being in March 1901. Awarded a benefit match in 1902, he was appointed as Rangers' reserve team coach in 1908.

The Broughton Rangers team during March 1892 with club captain Jerry Jackson (with ball) seated centre. The Rangers were approaching the end of their final season at Walness before transferring to Wheater's Field. Despite improvements that included the erection of a popular side stand in 1890 (holding over 6,000), the club, whose derby matches with Broughton were sarcastically dubbed 'the championship of the Lake District', due to the imposition of the River Irwell, decided it was time to move on.

two

Broughton Rangers at Wheater's Field

Broughton Rangers transferred to a site in Lower Broughton, commonly known as Wheater's Field, for 1892/93. The land, which belonged to the Deane Family (Tom Deane being a former Broughton and Lancashire RU player), was converted from 'a cinder bed to a grassy surface'. The infertile nature of the ground became evident as the playing area gained a reputation for its lack of grass although, after the first season, a local scribe declared it a 'perfect paradise in comparison to the death trap (Walness) at the other side of the river'.

Wheater's Field proved a fine talisman for the Rangers and their twenty-year residence provided the high points in the club's history. The strength of the side was in their mighty pack (they became famed for signing outstanding Cumbrian forwards), although they had several excellent backs, in particular Frank Harry, Andy Hogg and Bob Wilson.

When the historic meeting at the George Hotel, Huddersfield, took place on 29 August 1895, signalling the formation of the breakaway Northern Union, Broughton Rangers was the only local club to immediately join the rebels, Salford and Swinton resisting for another year. In the earlier years, the Northern Union separated its clubs into Lancashire and Yorkshire championships, Rangers winning the 'Red Rose' competition in 1896/97 (the club's first silverware) and 1898/99. When the leading outfits merged into one championship in 1901/02, the Rangers again triumphed adding the Challenge Cup to complete the sports first 'double'. The Challenge Cup returned to Wheater's Field in 1911, sandwiching the club's first Lancashire Cup success of 1906.

Wheater's Field itself, despite its shortcomings, proved a popular choice for the sport's major occasions and it hosted the finals of the Northern Union Challenge Cup (in 1907), the Championship (1910 and 1911), and Lancashire Cup (seven times, including the inaugural 1905 final). Representative matches were also allocated, England meeting Wales in December 1908 – the only international played at the ground – and Lancashire staging seven county matches there from 1896 to 1907.

In the summer of 1912, it was announced that 'considerable increases in ground rental and rates have at last compelled the present executive to seek a fresh enclosure'. Wheater's Field was also decaying and considered 'a battered, scarred old ground, hemmed in on all sides by houses' with 'a playing pitch as hard as nails and not a blade of grass to be seen', the grandstand (at the Lower Broughton Road end) having 'long wooden seats of a primitive age'. The last match at the ground took place on 9 April 1913, the visitors being St Helens. Today, the site of the Wheater's Field ground is covered by a housing estate, its location being traceable through the naming of Wheater's Crescent, Wheater's Street and Wheater's Terrace.

Welsh international brothers David (right) and Evan James joined Broughton Rangers in 1892, causing a sensation in rugby circles. They were an innovative pair who developed half-back play into the specialist roles we know today with David, the eldest by three years, feeding the scrums. They played four times for Rangers during October until, belatedly, their 'transfer' was rejected at a Lancashire RU meeting on the 22 October for alleged 'professionalism' after claims the Rangers paid them 30 shillings a week. With no one willing to decide their fate the matter passed through the hands of the Welsh and English RU's before (on 27 January 1893) the International Board suspended them for three years although, on appeal by Rangers, they did play twice during December, pending a final decision. Reinstated as amateurs in 1896, they returned to their previous club, Swansea, again playing for Wales, dazzling England on 14 January 1899, despite Evan breaking a collarbone! Within twelve days, they were back at Broughton taking their family of sixteen, including parents and three younger rugby-playing brothers! Having reached their thirties, David managed 13 matches and Evan 19 over the next two years, their siblings making greater contributions. Sadly, Evan died in August 1901 from consumption, after catching a severe cold playing for Rangers' reserves in October 1900.

It was also in 1892 that the Grosvenor Hotel, on the corner of Great Clowes Street and Clarence Street, became the club's new headquarters following their move to Wheater's Field, prompting one journalist to announce: 'The old "Mrs Boardman's Boys" are now Mrs Boardman's no longer!' Previously, the Bridge Inn on Lower Broughton Road had served as the Rangers' headquarters during their years at Walness and the players were known, affectionately, as 'Mrs Boardman's Boys' after Isabella Boardman, who ran the hostelry from 1881 to 1887. Club president Thomas Smith added: 'Might she long be spared to visit her boys in their new ground'. When she passed away in 1894, the president again acknowledged her warming influence saying 'She was with the members on every occasion and if they were in need of money, and at the time they sometimes were, though they are better off now, they always found "Ma" ready to help'. Her legacy remained, and for years afterwards the team was referred to as 'Mrs Boardman's Boys'.

Right: Charlie Thompson – known affectionately towards the end of his career as 'Owd Charlie' – was one of several players who made the transition from Rugby Union to Northern Union whilst with the Rangers. Having joined the club from Ulverston in 1893, his final match came in 1904 after 198 appearances under Northern Union rules. The highlight of his career was in 1901/02 when he was a member of the side that won the League championship and Challenge Cup. A forward, acknowledged by one scribe as 'a leading spirit noted for sterling work', he made the first of 3 Lancashire appearances against Yorkshire at Halifax in November 1899.

Below: Broughton Rangers pose in front of one of the goalposts at the commencement of the 1894/95 season, destined to be their last as members of the Rugby Union, with team captain J.A. Squires seated centre. It was to prove a good season results-wise, with 20 victories and 6 draws (from 36 matches) being their best return to date, winger George Berry contributing 18 tries.

Sam James – like elder brothers David and Evan – was a half-back, described by one writer at the time as 'energetic and determined'. Travelling north with the rest of the family in 1899, when just sixteen, he made his debut on 18 February that year in a home fixture with Tyldesley, partnering brother David (making his comeback match for the Rangers). Sam had previously played for Danycraig and Swansea, and was reserve for Wales on one occasion. He was to make 271 appearances for Broughton Rangers, the last being in 1908, representing Lancashire on 11 occasions and Other Nationalities twice. Stricken with poor health, he was given a benefit match in November 1908 to assist his recovery, but, tragically, suffered the same fate as brother Evan, in that he died at an early age from consumption, in March 1909.

George Ruddick wrote his name into the history books as far a Broughton Rangers was concerned, his 422 career appearances being a club record by some distance. Noted as 'one of the fastest forwards and most devastating tacklers to play the game' he earned recognition for Great Britain, Wales (he was born in Brecon) and was also claimed by Lancashire. In 1910, he had the distinction of being the club's first tourist to Australia and New Zealand. He missed the 1902 Challenge Cup final victory over Salford through injury after playing in all the previous rounds, but made amends as a member of the side that defeated Wigan in the 1911 final. He was also in the team that defeated Warrington in the 1906 Lancashire Cup decider. His lengthy Rangers career spanned the years 1899 to 1915, the First World War (during which he was badly wounded in the foot serving his country) bringing it to an end.

Frank Harry was signed from Torquay Athletic in 1899, having previously represented Devon county. Initially recruited as a full-back, he developed into an outstanding centre, a position he occupied as a member of the team that completed the League and Cup 'double' in 1901/02. He was described in the press as 'a gentleman player' – an attribute that must have made the awarding of a testimonial (in 1909) a popular decision. As well as putting in 213 appearances for the Rangers (the last in October 1909), and representing Lancashire 3 times, he demonstrated his sporting versatility through playing county cricket for Lancashire.

Billy Winskill is unique in that his 350 appearances for the Rangers includes a place in the club's two Challenge Cup-winning line-ups of 1902 and 1911. Born in Penrith in 1877, he first played rugby as a fifteen-year-old for Penrith Juniors and had spells with Penrith United and Percy Park (Northumberland) before arriving at Wheater's Field in August 1899. Having had his playing career disrupted by the First World War, he returned for a final 12 matches during 1919/20, when well into his forties. Weighing in at 14 stone 10 pounds, and almost six feet tall, he was a speedy forward who, according to one description, ran 'with knees up and arms flailing'. His county career also had longevity and he represented Cumberland 16 times from 1905 until 1919.

Broughton Rangers spread the net far and wide during the early years of the twentieth century in their search for talent. In Andy Hogg, recruited from Hawick in January 1899, they certainly struck gold, the powerful Scottish wingman becoming a great favourite with the Wheater's Field crowd, where he was known as 'The Braw Laddie'. He formed a formidable partnership with his centre and captain, Bob Wilson, crossing for a club record 186 tries during his 339 outings in the Rangers' colours before his final appearance in April 1910. He was selected by the Northern Union for the First Test against New Zealand at Headingley in 1908, and made three other international appearances: Other Nationalities against England (1909) and, rather surprisingly, England against New Zealand and Wales (both 1908). He was also adopted by Lancashire, who picked him on 15 occasions. The highlight of his club career was scoring a try in the 1902 Challenge Cup final demolition of neighbours Salford. He also appeared in the Lancashire Cup finals of 1906 and 1907, gaining a winners' medal in the former.

Encouraged by the success of Hogg, the Rangers returned to Scotland in 1900 to recruit his former Hawick team-mate, James Scott, the two being good friends having attended the same Hawick school. Although he had appeared in the three-quarter line whilst north of the border, it was in the pack that Scott established his reputation in the Northern Union, appearing in 145 matches for Broughton Rangers. His only representative honour came in January 1905 when he was in the Other Nationalities side that lost 26-11 to England at Park Avenue, Bradford.

Jim Trotter – born in Whitehaven in 1878 – was recruited from the Stockport Northern Union club in December 1901 and had a leading role in Rangers' completion of the 'double' in 1901/02. He missed the following campaign through making a return trip to South Africa, where he had worked previously as a gold miner (whilst continuing to play rugby), rejoining the Rangers for 1903/04. Described as a model forward with a powerful physique, he became the recognised pack leader and was club captain for a short period during 1906. Having represented Cheshire 6 times during the 1900-01 period (qualifying by virtue of playing for Stockport) he appeared in 4 matches for Lancashire (1904 to 1905), completing a rare 'set' with two matches for his native county, Cumberland, in 1907. Altogether, he played 126 times for Broughton Rangers and became a director of the club in 1913.

Billy Oram joined Broughton Rangers from Stockport at the same time as Trotter, both making their debut in the 1901 Boxing Day match at Hull. The loss of two such outstanding forwards hastened the demise of the struggling Cheshire club, who disbanded in 1903, having been founder members of the Northern Union in 1895. Born in Abercarn, Monmouthshire, Oram was regarded in his day as one of the cleverest foragers in the Northern Union with 'a gift of speed'. Like Trotter, he also qualified for Cheshire (8 times from 1899 to 1901) to which he added 4 Lancashire caps during the 1902/03 campaign. He played in 158 matches for the Rangers, his finale being in April 1908. He later played for local junior club, Pendleton.

Conservative MP, Mr F. Platt-Higgins (in the top hat), about to perform the kick off for Broughton Rangers in their opening match of the 1900/01 season at Wheater's Field against Warrington. His presence was no doubt geared at winning the hearts and minds of the Broughton contingent amongst the 6,000 attendance as a General Election was taking place a few days later! His strategy worked, retaining his seat for the North Salford Division (which covered Broughton) as the Tory party was re-elected. Played on 29 September, Rangers also claimed victory in this match, with a narrow 6-5 win through tries from star three-quarters Andy Hogg and Bob Wilson.

Robert ('Bob') James Wilson was a natural successor to Harry Chapman. Born in Carnforth, he joined Rangers at the beginning of the 1900/01 season. A quick centre with a neat sidestep, he was, like his predecessor, noted for good conduct on and off the field – qualities that earned him the captaincy of the Rangers (for a club record nine seasons) and his former team, Morecambe. He also led Lancashire (with whom he appeared 16 times – the most by a Rangers player) and, in 1905, played for England against Other Nationalities. In 1901/02, he steered the Rangers to Championship and Challenge Cup success, scoring a cup final record three tries in the latter (a 25-0 win over Salford), later equalled, but not surpassed until Leeds' Leroy Rivett bagged four in the 1999 decider. It was during the 1901/02 season that Wilson scored a club record 33 tries (which was never bettered), his overall total of 141 being second only to that of Andy Hogg. Further success came when he led Rangers to victory in the 1906 Lancashire Cup final. Wilson broke a collarbone in a home match with Leeds during September 1908, virtually ending his career. He made several more appearances but his form had deserted him, his last match being in December 1909. After retirement, his health declined and he passed away in February 1916 aged thirty-eight.

BROUGHTON RANGERS v OLDHAM

A caricature of the Broughton Rangers *v*. Oldham match at Wheater's Field on 8 March 1902, which features Harry Woodhead's opening try and the first of Willie James' two goals in a 16-5 win. The two clubs were amongst the most powerful in the early years of the Northern Union, and the victory took the Rangers a step closer to the 1901/02 championship, which they had effectively wrapped up in February, so great was their lead over second-placed Salford, who eventually finished 12 points behind.

Known as 'Fearless' Jack Beetham, the industrious forward represented Askam (his hometown club), Dalton, Barrow and Millom before linking up with Broughton Rangers in 1902. He made one international appearance, in January 1908 at Central Park, Wigan, when selected by England against the New Zealand tourists. He was more popular with the county selectors, however, and picked 5 times by Lancashire and 11 by Cumberland (including 9 whilst with Millom). Beetham's final Rangers' match in 1922 was his 374th appearance for the club, second only to contemporary, George Ruddick. He shared a benefit in 1922 with George Davidson, who arrived from Apatria in 1910 and was full-back in the 1911 Challenge Cup final.

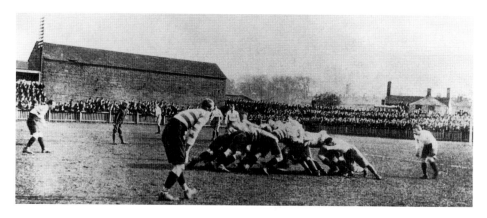

A scrum-down at Lawkholme Lane, Keighley, as the home side take on Broughton Rangers in the first round of the 1902 Northern Union Challenge Cup on 15 March. Amongst those awaiting developments are Rangers winger Andy Hogg (closest to the camera) and Keighley half-back Harold Myers (far right). The Rangers triumphed 15-7 in front of 5,957 spectators on their way to winning the trophy for the first time.

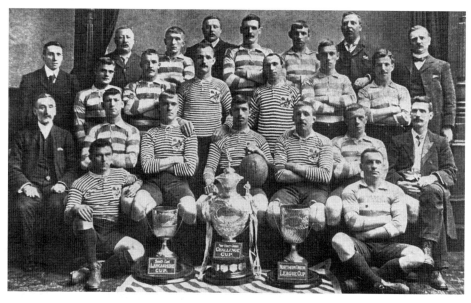

The official photograph commemorating Broughton Rangers' domination of the 1901/02 season. From left to right, back row: Tom Royle (trainer), Charlie Thompson, Ernie Gresty (ex-secretary), Jim Trotter, Billy Winskill, J.E. Kirkham (president), G.H. Jones (junior vice-president). Third row, standing: Fred Fearnley (secretary), Arthur Widdeson, John Stead, George Ruddick, Sam James, Jack Fielding, Frank Harry. Seated: W. Isherwood (treasurer), Jim Garrity, Andy Hogg, Bob Wilson (captain), George Whitehead, Billy Oram, C. Hough (senior vice-president). On floor: Willie James, Alf Barrett. Being the first season of the Northern League Championship (having replaced the county leagues) the trophy was still being made, the cup on the right being a substitute! The South East Lancashire Cup (on left) was a short-lived, six-team league competition, Rangers finishing two points ahead of neighbours Swinton.

Record breaker Billy Harris was born in Rainscough and, having played for Pendleton Britannia, was 'discovered' representing Glover's Cable Works in a local workshops competition. In making 302 appearances for the Rangers, he was used in several back positions including full-back and stand-off half, but it was from the three-quarter line – at wing and centre – where his speed and eye for an opening brought most of his 123 tries. A regular marksman, he added 233 goals, contributing towards a club points record for a career (835), a season (243 in 1906/07) and a match (32 at Liverpool City in September 1906). In the latter, he equalled half-back Joe Nelson's record – set in March 1899 in a home Challenge Cup tie with Rothwell – of scoring 10 goals in a match. Harris, who was club captain in 1912/13, continued to play until 1915 when the First World War intervened. He played twice for Lancashire in 1912.

Robert 'Bob' Watkins Poole (illustrated here) and JH Jewitt are the only England Rugby Union internationals signed by the Rangers, having received one cap each in 1896 and 1902, respectively. The Durham-born pair both arrived from Hartlepool Rovers during 1903. Jewitt, a forward, was the first to appear, in January, but he managed only eleven games in a ten-month career. Poole, a full-back who made his debut in September, proved more successful, appearing in 99 matches over four seasons. A former captain of the Durham county RU side, he was selected 6 times for Lancashire under the Northern Union banner and, in 1905, played once for England.

Above: Baines' cards – printed in full colour – first appeared in the 1880s and were available up to the time of the First World War. Produced by John Baines of Bradford, they sold in packets of six and were a popular collectors' item for young supporters. The Broughton Rangers cards reproduced on this page are from the early 1900s and feature two of the clubs outstanding players of that period; Bob Wilson (above left) and George Ruddick (above right).

Opposite below: Willie (left) and Claude James were the younger brothers of David, Evan and Sam. When the family moved north in 1899, Willie was fourteen and Claude ten. Willie was another off the James' conveyor-belt of half-backs, being full of tricks and renowned for his 'daring' defence. Following his debut in the opening match of the 1899/1900 season, he appeared in 183 matches for the Rangers, kicking 148 goals. He also represented Lancashire and Other Nationalities. After losing form and being dropped during March 1906, he was placed on the transfer list at his own request, subsequently disappearing from the scene until making a surprise return for the 1909 Christmas Day clash with Salford. Claude was different in stature to his four pint-sized older brothers and described as the 'big boy' of the family. Better suited to the three-quarter line, he made his first appearance there at Rochdale in December 1905 with Sam and Willie at half-back. In 131 matches he scored 85 goals and 46 tries, including a club record 6 against Liverpool City in October 1906, emulated by Walter Scott (in 1913) and Clifford Mills (1934). Willie and Claude transferred to Leigh in October 1910, the two being listed at £150 each.

Right: Alf Barrett had demonstrated his worth as an outstanding centre during seven seasons with Salford before being approached by Broughton Rangers on their entry into the Northern Union in 1895. For Barrett, it was a good move, culminating in him receiving a benefit in 1905, after playing in 235 matches for the Rangers, the last in September 1904. He was in the team that won the Lancashire League titles of 1896/97 and 1898/99, and a member of the side that won the Championship and Challenge Cup in 1901/02, although missing the final of the latter (having played in all but one of the previous rounds) when Willie James returned from injury. Barrett was elected Rangers captain for 1899/1900 – a role he had fulfilled at Salford. He later played for the Pendleton Britannia club.

Forwards James Lamb 'Jim' Clampitt (left) and Richard 'Dick' Clampitt, seen here in pre-Rangers days, were another brotherly duo to make an impact with Broughton Rangers, both being born in, and playing for, Millom. Jim – a real handful for opponents – was 'strong and vigorous', whilst Dick (an inch taller than his elder brother at 5ft 10ins) was 'brilliant in mauls and fast in the loose'. Their level of commitment to Broughton Rangers was demonstrated when both were dismissed (in separate incidents) in the match against the Australian tourists in February 1909, their eleven colleagues holding on heroically to win 14-12. Both represented Cumberland, Jim's 21 matches being the most county appearances by any player whilst attached to Broughton Rangers, adding to the 3 he made whilst with Millom. Jim gained the higher profile through 3 Test appearances, 6 matches for England and a place on the 1914 tour Down Under. Jim played 269 matches for Rangers and Dick 213, the pair being in the successful 1911 Challenge Cup side and Jim having a place in the 1906 Lancashire Cup-winning team.

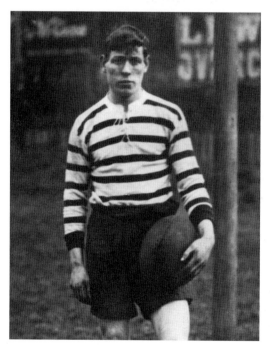

W.H. 'Billy' Barlow was a local lad who joined Broughton Rangers in 1905, having played for junior sides Salford Trinity and Prestwich Institute. His regular position was full-back, although he appeared mostly in the three-quarters and at half-back towards the end of his career. Overlooked for representative honours, he played in 286 matches for Broughton, the last in 1920, kicking 127 goals. He was at full-back in the club's Lancashire Cup final teams of 1906 and 1907, his crowning moment being at stand-off for the 1911 Challenge Cup final victory over Wigan.

Lancashire's club captains 'celebrate' receiving home draws in the first round of the Northern Union (later 'Rugby League') Challenge Cup in March 1907, led by Salford's Jimmy Lomas (fourth from right), Broughton Rangers' Bob Wilson (third from right) and Swinton's Billy Simister (extreme right). It was Warrington, by virtue of defeating Oldham in the final at Wheater's Field, who would sing longest. The Rangers had beaten Warrington 15-6 in the Lancashire Cup final at Wigan the previous December (their first success in the competition), their pack controlling a match described as 'not pretty'. Hopes of further glory in the Challenge Cup crashed in the second round when the visiting Leeds side won 11-7.

The Broughton Rangers team prior to winning 8-0 at Swinton on 14 September 1907. From left to right, back row: Fred Hardyman, Albert Gendle, C.J. Darlison, Jim Trotter, J. Grainey, J. Jackson, Andy Hogg. Front row: Billy Winskill, George Ruddick, Bob Wilson (captain), Jack Flynn, Billy Barlow, Jack Beetham. Two months later, the Rangers appeared in their second consecutive Lancashire Cup final, but were unable to retain their prize, losing 16-9 to Oldham at Rochdale.

Official Programme.

NEW ZEALAND

VERSUS

BROUGHTON
RANGERS

.. at ..

WHEATER'S FIELD,
LOWER BROUGHTON.

On Saturday, October 19, 1907

Left: The outer cover of the programme for the Broughton Rangers match against the New Zealanders during 1907 – the first international tour undertaken after the formation of the Northern Union. The attendance, reported in at least one newspaper as 24,000 (which would constitute a ground record for Wheater's Field if correct), was almost certainly closer to 20,000. (The following March, a Challenge Cup tie at the ground against Warrington was watched by 21,273, drawing the comment that 'when the All Blacks (New Zealand) played the gate was about 20,000, on this occasion it was eclipsed'.) Either way, it was the second highest crowd of the visitors' gruelling 35-game schedule.

 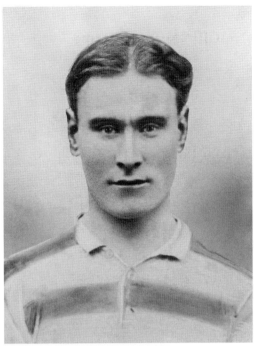

Above left: Walter Cheetham made his first appearance for the Rangers in February 1909, although it was not until the 1912/13 season that he established himself as a regular in the pack. A member of the 1920 Lancashire Cup-winning team, he played 138 times for the club, his final outing being in 1923.

Above right: W.J. Larkin was signed from the Weaste club in Salford, making his debut in a club record 59-0 Challenge Cup win over Barton in March 1913, at Wheater's Field. Like Cheetham, he was a forward who waited several seasons – until 1919/20 – to stake a regular place, the First World War limiting his opportunities until then. He was another member of the successful 1920 Lancashire Cup side, playing for the club on 166 occasions (the last of them being in 1927). He was club captain in 1920/21 and 1921/22 and appeared twice for Lancashire. The two photographs reproduced on this page appeared in the Pinnace collection of 1923 (see chapter five).

Opposite below: Broughton Rangers players before a pre-season public trial at Wheater's Field in August 1908, the 'Stripes' (first-team backs, reserve forwards) taking on the 'Whites' (first-team forwards, reserve backs). The two captains (centre with match balls) are George Ruddick (white) and Bob Wilson (hoops). The stocky chap (third row, third player from left) is Reuben Glaskie, referred to as 'a heavyweight forward'. A stalwart of the Rangers 'A' (reserve) team, he played as an unpaid amateur in a fourteen-year Rangers career that ended in 1919 when he joined the Trafford & Clayton junior side. Later he made a big impact as a member of the Rangers' board – along with chairman Fred Kennedy, Harry Rebbitt (who brought the James brothers back to the club in 1899) and Captain Stuart Hampson – that worked tirelessly to keep the club afloat during the years at The Cliff. Glaskie was one of several Jewish players who appeared for Broughton Rangers, the club being located amongst one of many Jewish neighbourhoods established in the late 1800s as immigrants arrived from Eastern Europe. Remarking on his passing in 1956, a friend paid tribute to the Jewish community 'without whom the Rangers would have disappeared long ago'.

Jim Clampitt became club captain in 1910/11, leading the Rangers to their second Challenge Cup victory that season. The success came at the climax of the club's first season as a limited liability company: on 6 August 1910 they had become The Broughton Rangers Football Club Limited, registered with capital of £2,000 in 10 shilling shares 'to acquire and take over business assets and liability of present incorporated club known as The Broughton Rangers Football Club'. The first chairman was Fred Kennedy.

The official photograph in honour of Broughton Rangers winning the 1911 Challenge Cup. From left to right, back row: Robert Holland, William Larkin, Edgar Heys, Harry Rebbitt, Fred Kennedy (chairman), Fred Fearnley (secretary), Hilderick Bouch, Louis Fraser. Third row: E. Hill, Arkle Hirst, Jim Gorry, Billy Winskill, Dick Clampitt, Fred Robinson, H. Taylor, George Fearnehough. Second row, seated: John Gatenby, Alfred Wild, Jim Clampitt (captain), Billy Harris, George Ruddick, John Errington. Front row, on floor: William Booth, George Davidson, Ned Jones, Billy Barlow, Walter Scott. Inset: Thomas Cooper, Edwin Mather. The Rangers defeated favourites Wigan 4-0 in the final at The Willows, Salford, through two penalty goals from Harris, on a pitch that resembled a quagmire due to heavy rain.

three

Fallowfield Stadium

Fallowfield Stadium, situated near Old Hall Lane, was built for Manchester Athletic Club who transferred from Old Trafford in 1892 due to the Manchester Ship Canal development. It could accommodate athletics and track cycling.

At that time, Manchester lacked a venue capable of accommodating large crowds and Fallowfield came into its own. The Football Association staged the 1893 Wolverhampton v. Everton FA Cup final there in front of a new Cup final record crowd of 45,000. The biggest sporting event seen in Manchester until then, it was marred by crowd trouble, several skirmishes taking place, including battles with police as they valiantly tried to restore order. The experience discouraged the FA from staging further finals, although they allocated a semi-final replay between Liverpool and Sheffield United to the venue in 1899. The Monday afternoon game attracted 30,000, but further difficulty occurred with congestion at the entrances and, with spectators encroaching the playing area, the match was abandoned at half-time. It was the last time the FA used the enclosure.

The first high-profile rugby match was in December 1894 when Lancashire met Cheshire, several county games being held over the next few years. In March 1897, the England v. Scotland Calcutta Cup clash was staged although it was the last time a Rugby Union 'International Championship' fixture was held in the north of England and another hundred years before England again played in the Manchester area.

The Northern Union took two Challenge Cup finals to Fallowfield. The first was the 1899 decider between Hunslet and Oldham. To avoid repeating the FA Cup semi-final fiasco of a few weeks earlier, more entrances (26) were available with a large police force (mounted and on foot) present. Things went smoothly, although Salford and Swinton, unhappy at neither of them being allocated the final, arranged to meet in a counter attraction. Eventually a plea from the Lancashire NU committee resulted in them playing the previous evening. Ironically, Salford and Swinton met at Fallowfield in the 1900 final, an event planned for Wheater's Field but re-scheduled after the NU Committee subsequently inspected the ground, deciding (incorrectly as it proved) it could not accommodate the anticipated crowd. Fallowfield soon fell out of favour for big matches, although over the years it has provided a home for several Rugby Union clubs, including the much-travelled Broughton Park.

In 1934, the stadium pre-empted Manchester's 2002 staging of the Commonwealth Games when it hosted that year's cycling events. The main games (then known as the British Empire Championships) took place at London's White City Stadium. It was renamed 'The Reg Harris Stadium' at the start of the 1950s, in honour of the five-times world sprint cycling champion who dominated the early post-war years. The stadium was demolished in 1994 and is now the site of the Vice-Chancellor's Court for Manchester University.

Fallowfield Stadium, seen from the air during a well-attended meeting in 1924. The banked cycling track can be seen around the perimeter with the athletics track inside.

A newspaper cutting of the 1893 FA Cup final between Everton and Wolverhampton Wanderers at Fallowfield. Although it was a record attendance for the final, the picture gives an indication of the difficulty for many spectators in seeing the game.

NORTHERN UNION CHALLENGE CUP.

THE FINAL TIE.

OLDHAM v. HUNSLET.

BRILLIANT VICTORY OF THE LANCASTRIANS.

Held at Fallowfield on 29 April 1899, the third final of the Northern Union Challenge Cup was the first to take place outside of Yorkshire, the others having been staged at Headingley, Leeds. Favourites Oldham had an early fright and trailed Hunslet by nine points shortly before the interval, eventually overcoming the formidable, but tiring, Hunslet pack in the second period to win the trophy 19-9.

The 1899 Oldham team with the Challenge Cup. From left to right, back row: Bob Edwards, James Moffatt, Emanuel Bonser, Herbert Ellis, Arthur Lees (captain), Harry Broome, Joe Lees, George Frater. Seated: Tom Fletcher, Tom Sellars, Dicky Thomas, Sam Lees, Tom Davies. Front row: Tom Martin, Sam Williams, Joe Lawton, William Barnes.

THE LION RAMPANT.

Left: The Lion of Swinton triumphed in the 1900 final played on 28 April at Fallowfield, when Salford was defeated in an all-Manchester affair. Tied 8-8 at half-time, Swinton won 16-8, their brilliant back division taking command after the break, inspired by their captain Jim Valentine, who played on despite dislocating a shoulder during the first half.

Below: Swinton's team and officials with the Northern Union Challenge Cup in 1900. From left to right, back row: G. Whitman, Dick Jones, J. Butterworth. Third row: T. Worthington, J. Cooper, Jack Evans, Jack Preston, Evan Vigors, Charlie Pollitt, J. Sharples, Ben Murphy. Second row: R.J. Hampson, Bob Tickle, Vernon Hampson, Bob Valentine, Jim Valentine (captain), Bob Messer, Jack Lewis, Alf Chorley, C. Platt, George Harris. Front row: J. Scholes, J. Mills, Joe Morgan, Dai Davies, W.J. Widdowson, H. Murray.

four

Salford and The Willows

Salford moved to The Willows, situated in the Weaste district, in 1901, having received notice to quit New Barnes (their base since 1878) to make way for the expanding Manchester Ship Canal complex. The New Barnes Estate was also the site of Manchester Racecourse (covering virtually the length of Trafford Road), racing transferring to Castle Irwell (also in Salford) from 1902.

Salford's New Barnes ground had been allocated only one county fixture (Lancashire meeting Yorkshire in November 1898) whereas The Willows quickly became popular with the Northern Union authorities for hosting major occasions. The estimated capacity of 25,000 helped make it the leading rugby venue in the Manchester area during the early 1900s and a timely replacement for the much-maligned Fallowfield.

The first of ten county matches played at The Willows took place in November 1902, a Lancashire v. Yorkshire 'Roses' clash that brought in 14,000 spectators. This was followed with the staging of four major finals in eight seasons: the Northern Union Challenge Cup of 1904 and 1911, and the Championship in 1908 and 1909. From 1912 until 1924, the Lancashire committee deemed The Willows the perfect choice for their county cup final and seven were allocated during this period, 25,000 watching the 1920 decider between Broughton Rangers and Leigh. The most prestigious event though was the decisive Third Test between the Northern Union (effectively Great Britain) and Australia in January 1922, which drew an estimated 21,000.

Following its selection for the 1926 Challenge Cup semi-final between Oldham and Wigan Highfield, The Willows was displaced as Manchester's number one venue in the late 1920s by Swinton's new, spacious Station Road ground. With the exception of an England v. Wales international in 1932, it was almost forty years before it came back into favour, its profile boosted by the exciting ground improvements taking place at that time under the chairmanship of Brian Snape – including a first-rate social club and floodlighting. The ascendancy of the Salford team during this period meant spectator interest was high and the terraces usually full. From 1968 until 1979, it was used for several important fixtures, including five internationals and three cup finals: the Player's No.6 Trophy, the Captain Morgan Trophy and the Lancashire Cup. The latter between Widnes and Workington Town in 1979 was to be the last 'big match' staged at the ground.

Salford themselves have given their fans two outstanding sides during their time at The Willows: the 1930s team managed by Lance Todd and the late 1960s/early 1970s outfit featuring 'Welsh Wizard' David Watkins. At the time of writing, there are exciting plans to move the team, now known as the Salford City Reds, to a new 20,000 capacity (mostly seated) all-covered stadium, at Barton.

The famous Salford 'Red Devils' team at The Willows in 1938, at the peak of their success. From left to right, back row: Billy Williams, Joe Bradbury, Dai Davies, Bert Day, Harold Thomas, Paddy Dalton, Jack Feetham. Seated: Albert Gear, Barney Hudson, Alan Edwards, Lance Todd (manager), Gus Risman (captain), Bob Brown, Harold Osbaldestin. Front: Billy Watkins, Sammy Miller. The 1930s brought 3 League Championships, 5 Lancashire Championships, 4 Lancashire Cup wins and a Challenge Cup victory.

The Salford team at Featherstone Rovers before a Challenge Cup tie on 28 January 1973. From left to right, back row: Johnny Ward, Maurice Richards, Graham MacKay, Tony Colloby, Paul Charlton, Alan Grice, Ellis Devlin. Front row: Ken Gill, Doug Davies, Chris Hesketh, David Watkins (captain), Peter Banner, Colin Dixon. Richards appears amused by the 'crown' placed on the head of 'King' Watkins by a supporter! Salford had returned to Wembley in 1969 after a thirty-year gap and looked set to emulate the success of their 1930s predecessors. In the event, the side won two Championships, plus the BBC2 Floodlit Trophy and Lancashire Cup once each, whilst playing some spectacular rugby.

Above: Colin Dixon scores for Salford in their 20-7 Challenge Cup quarter-final win over Widnes at The Willows in March 1969. The side were destined for Wembley. Other Salford players are Martin Dickens (9) and Jackie Brennan (7). The attendance of 18,825 was the highest recorded at the ground since the 1950s.

Left: David Watkins (left) and Keith Fielding – two Salford record-breakers in action at Swinton's Station Road ground during the 1976 Premiership Trophy final defeat to St Helens. Watkins' 221 goals and 493 points in 1972/73, and Fielding's return of 46 tries in 1973/74 are both club records.

Left: The Northern Union Challenge Cup final was held at The Willows for the first time in April 1904, Halifax defeating Warrington 8-3. The cartoon strip here features the two Halifax tries by centre Joe Riley and scrum-half Jack Morley who, as captain, is depicted lifting the trophy (top left), whilst a colleague performs cartwheels in the background!

Below: The second and last Challenge Cup final taken to The Willows was the 1911 meeting of Broughton Rangers and Wigan during April. Wigan, having recorded an emphatic 'double' over the Rangers during the season, were overwhelming favourites, but the pitch – turned into a mud bath after torrential rain (which also kept the crowd down to a paltry 8,000) – proved a great leveller, the Rangers' powerful pack taking command to grind out a surprise 4-0 victory.

The first Championship final at Weaste was in 1908 when League leaders Oldham took on second-placed Hunslet on a scorching hot day in May. A closely-fought match ended level at 7-7, Hunslet winning the replay 12-2 seven days later at Wakefield. It was their fourth trophy of the season.

A postcard showing the Wigan team with their collection of silverware from the 1908/09 season including their Championship prize (second trophy from left), having beaten Oldham 7-3 in the final at The Willows during May 1909.

FROM OUR OBSERVATION POST.
Salford v. Broughton Rangers.

Broughton Rangers have now got a pair of legs just like Danson's to fill his shoes.

Those of Barnes have a tendency to turn the other way.

Kelly was the only man to cross the line, & he left the ball behind, in his hurry.

Larkin, the Rangers captain.

The referee danced artistically through the afternoon

This linesman had no ambition in that direction

LUCKET PUR

An ice-cream vendor was in attendance to keep the spectators cool — quite unnecessary.

Salford and Broughton Rangers fought out a scoreless draw at The Willows on 18 March 1922, the closest to scoring apparently being the Rangers Tommy Kelly, who appeared on the wing in this match. Centre Jimmy Barnes joined the Rangers from Egerton in 1911, his final appearance being in 1927 after 237 matches. His biggest day was the 1920 Lancashire Cup win, and he subsequently replaced Tom Danson as captain for the rest of that season after Danson's career ending injury in that match. Amazingly, 'Lucketti's Pure Ices' continued to be sold around the Willows ground until the mid-1960s.

Broughton Rangers loose-forward Jack Price (standing, third player from right) made his Great Britain Test debut at Headingley, Leeds, on 1 October 1921, becoming the first Rangers player selected since 1914. Britain won this opening match of the series 6-5, securing the Ashes in the decisive Third Test at The Willows the following January. Warrington forward Billy Cunliffe (standing, player on left) joined Rangers in 1930, although he only appeared twice for the club.

Broughton Rangers v. Hull.

BROUGHTON'S VICTORY OVER SALFORD.

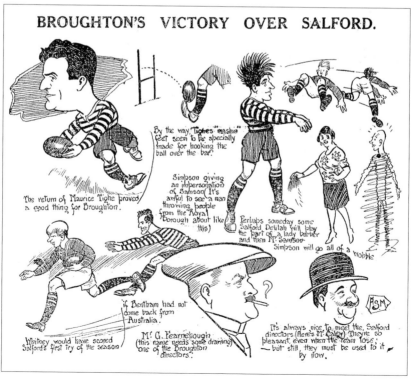

Above: Broughton Rangers line-up at the start of the 1924/25 season. From left to right, back row: H. Taylor (trainer), Jim Curran, L.J. Slater, W.J. Larkin, Jim Scott, Arthur McGhie, (unknown). Seated: Tommy Kelly, E.G. Morrison, Frank Lomas, Bill Wootton (captain), Danny Thomas, Jimmy Barnes. On ground: Edwin Battersby, Herbert Booth. Local lad Scott was signed in 1915 but, like many others, had his career put on hold due to the First World War. He eventually played an 'official' game for the Rangers at Salford during January 1919, the first of 214 over the next eleven seasons. A forward, considered a 'rare scrimmager', he was a member of the side that won the Lancashire Cup in 1920. He was the younger brother of three-quarter Walter Scott, who made 158 appearances in Rangers' colours between 1910 and 1920 (including the 1911 Challenge Cup final).

Opposite above: Broughton Rangers met Hull at The Cliff in February 1923 in a Challenge Cup tie. The result (13-0 to Hull) was hardly surprising with the high-flying Humbersiders eventually finishing the season as League leaders and runners-up in the Challenge Cup. The Rangers were a struggling outfit and ended the campaign 24th of the 27 teams.

Opposite below: A derby clash between Broughton Rangers and Salford in September 1924, as depicted by a cartoon strip. In a season when both clubs were struggling in the lower third of the League, the Rangers won 11-0. The artist highlights the return to the club of stand-off Maurice Tighe (who contributed a try and goal) after an absence of over five years, having been with Oldham in the interim.

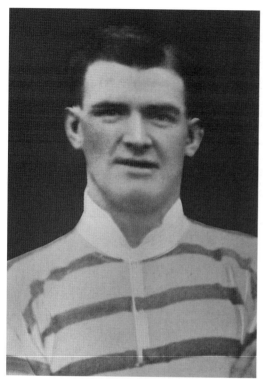

The four pictures reproduced on this and the facing page are from the Pinnace cigarette card series, first issued by Godfrey Phillips Ltd in 1923. There was an incredible total of 2,462 cards covering association football, rugby union and rugby league, including 13 featuring Rangers' players. Jim Curran (left) was born in Wigan having played for the Swinley Hornets club before making his debut for the Rangers in March 1921. Operating mostly at hooker he played in 239 matches for the club, joining Leigh in 1930. A steady performer, he was considered unlucky not to receive representative honours.

Billy Bentham was another product of Swinley Hornets. Born in Wigan, he was to play for the club 285 times before his farewell match in December 1929. He appeared mostly in the three-quarter line (usually on the wing) registering 112 tries for the club. Unlucky to miss the 1920 Lancashire Cup final triumph due to injury, he was elected club captain for the 1923/24 season and, following a two-year gap, took on that role again in 1926/27.

Welsh wing three-quarter M.S. Morgan
made his Rangers debut at The Cliff on
4 November 1922 against local rivals
Swinton, having signed from the Resolven
Rugby Union club, near Neath. He was to
appear in 21 matches over the next two
seasons, recording 4 tries.

Centre C. Rowlands joined the Rangers from the
Resolven club at the same time as M.S. Morgan,
the pair having travelled north together in October
1922. They had a joint-debut as a wing-pairing
following successful outings with the reserves. Like
his fellow Welshman, Rowlands played for just
two campaigns, covering 32 matches.

MONK'S IMPRESSIONS OF PROMINENT BROUGHTON RANGERS PLAYERS.

Left to right:—Mr. J. E. Hoey (Secretary, Broughton Rangers), G. L. Dixon, T. Kelly, G. Simpson (capt.), J. Curran, W. Bentham, and J. Finnerty.

Caricatures of Broughton Rangers personalities in 1925/26, depicting, from left to right: club secretary Jack Hoey, George Dixon, Tommy Kelly, George Simpson, Jim Curran, Billy Bentham and Jim Finnerty. Finnerty, a centre signed from Oldham, played just 16 times, all in the one season.

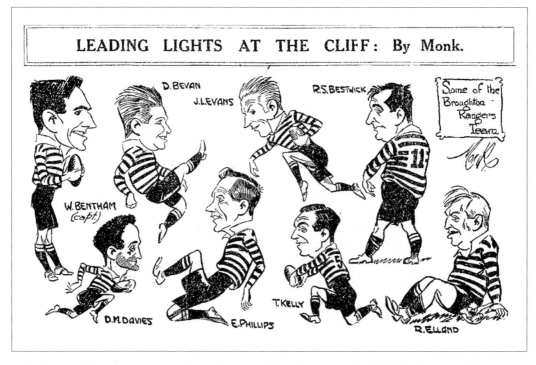

LEADING LIGHTS AT THE CLIFF: By Monk.

A further set of Rangers caricatures from the pen of 'Monk' appeared in 1926/27, featuring Billy Bentham, Dai Davies, Dan Bevan, Jack Evans, Evan Phillips, Tommy Kelly, R.S. Bestwick and R. Elland. Davies (a scrum-half), Bevan (full-back), Evans (wing) and Phillips (forward) all came from Welsh Rugby Union, former Llanelli player Evans having been capped for Wales. Davies, signed from Neath in January 1926, was destined to be a three-time Wembley loser with Warrington (1933), Huddersfield (1935) and Keighley (1937). Forwards Bestwick and Elland arrived from Weston-super-Mare and Clifton in Cumberland (as it was then known), respectively.

Above: The England *v.* Wales match on 6 April 1927 was the only international held at The Cliff (excepting the England *v.* France amateur game in 1952). This caricature features a try for Wales from Wigan's legendary wing Johnny Ring, created by Swinton's Billo Rees. It was England, however, who won a keenly fought contest 11–8.

Left: Joe Walsh was signed from local junior side Cadishead, making his first appearance for Rangers at home to Barrow in October 1929. Playing in the pack (mostly at hooker) he competed in 165 matches, the last being in April 1935.

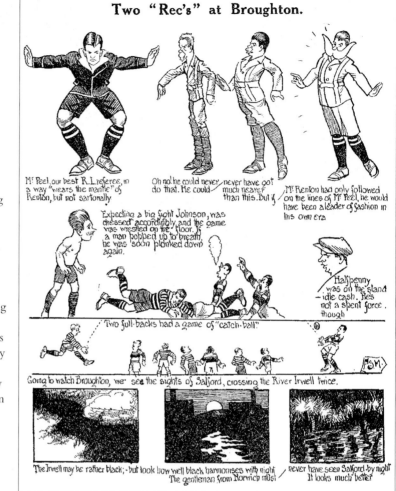

Two "Rec's" at Broughton.

Right: The title of this strip relates to the fact that Rangers were taking on visitors St Helens Recreation, popularly referred to as the 'Recs', and members of the Rugby League from 1919 until 1939. The match was in the opening round of the 1929 Challenge Cup, the Recs winning 13-2 on the way to a semi-final place where they lost narrowly to Wigan, missing out on being in the first final to be staged at Wembley. The artist seems particularly interested in the murky waters of the adjoining River Irwell.

Opposite above left: Full-back Llew Williams arrived from local rivals Salford during the 1930 close season, appearing in 110 games for the Rangers before deciding to retire in August 1933. He scored 94 goals for the club but was unable to add further representative honours to his two county caps with Glamorgan & Monmouthshire whilst at Salford. Williams signed from Crumlin Rugby Union club for Salford in 1927, where he was later joined by brother Billy, a Rugby League tourist in 1928 and 1932.

Opposite above right: Back-row forward George Bunter was described as a 'terrific player who never knew went to stop' but while his action-packed style meant that he was loved by the Rangers diehards, he was, to quote a contemporary journalist, 'hated by every other supporter'. Formerly with Hartlepool Rovers Rugby Union club (where he was capped for the Durham county side), he made his Rangers entrance in January 1932, playing 278 times in a lengthy career that ended in 1946. In November 1940 he appeared for England in a wartime international against Wales at Oldham.

Right: As can be seen from this caricature describing him as 'genial', long-term Rangers chairman Fred Kennedy was a popular personality. His first involvement was as a player over a six-year period during the Rugby Union era. Later, he took up refereeing and was in charge of Yorkshire's matches with Cumberland (at Workington in 1903) and Australia (Hull, 1908). His thirteen years as a referee ended when he took on the mantle of Rangers chairman in 1910 after it became a limited company – a role he held for 24 seasons, including the first one at Belle Vue. Elected chairman of the Rugby League for the 1928/29 season, he was rewarded for fifteen years service as member of the Northern Union Council through the presentation of a gold medal. Kennedy was a builders' merchant, his business being based in Lower Broughton.

The genial Mr. FRED KENNEDY, of Broughton Rangers, who has well earned his long service medal.

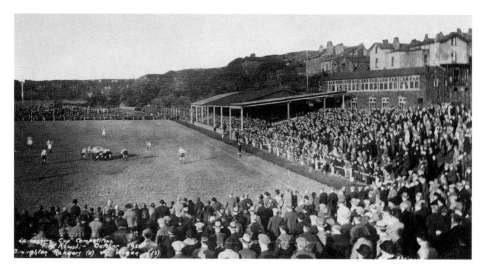

An excellent view of The Cliff on match day, clearly showing the grandstand (right) on the Lower Broughton Road side of the ground. The occasion was a first round Lancashire Cup match in October 1931, visitors Wigan winning 13-8.

Broughton Rangers reserves at The Cliff in September 1932, the start of the club's final season there. From left to right, back row: H. Fenby (trainer), William Shaw, Joe Whitehead, Wilf Foster, Harry Turner, Jack Tonge, E. Axon, Jimmy Barnes. Seated: J. Barlow, N. Cummings, Billy Doran (captain), A. Hilton, O. Britton. On ground: J. Fairclough, H. Barber. Cumbrian three-quarter Doran transferred to Salford in November 1929 in exchange for half-back Tommy Mannion and a substantial fee in a bid to ease the Rangers' financial plight. Doran did not replicate his Broughton form, however, and returned to The Cliff for a modest fee in 1931. The Rangers first team ended 1932/33 in 13th place (out of 28) in the League. Apart from finishing 9th in 1920/21, it was the best showing since the First World War. A low point was 1927/28 when the Rangers were one place off the bottom.

six

Swinton and Station Road

Swinton transferred to Station Road in 1929 when at their peak, having won all four major trophies on offer the previous season. The decision to purchase the land, which stood alongside the railway line, was made after a breakdown in negotiations with their existing landlord at Chorley Road, their home since 1887.

The new ground covered almost 8 acres with an estimated capacity for around 45,000 spectators (reportedly double that of their former enclosure). It certainly captured the imagination of one scribe who wrote that the 'first impression of Swinton's new ground was its vast area. That cramped appearance of Chorley Road disappeared when I viewed the ground from the top of the mound on the Popular Side.' Station Road opened for the first time in March when Swinton entertained Wigan, instantly taking over as the venue for major Rugby League events in the Manchester area.

Whereas the Northern Union/Rugby League authorities had taken just three county matches to Chorley Road, Station Road was allocated its first big match within a month of opening. The occasion was the 1929 St Helens Recreation-Wigan Challenge Cup semi-final, the new enclosure passing the test with flying colours. The match attracted 31,000 spectators, a new record for that stage of the competition, surpassed a year later when 37,169 entered to see the St Helens versus Wigan semi-final. In January 1930, the Third Test against Australia took place at Station Road, another 'bumper' attendance of 34,709 setting a record for a Test in Britain.

With such returns it was little wonder that Station Road monopolised the region's important matches. In a period that extended to well over half a century, it hosted 15 Tests (plus 4 other internationals), an incredible 30 Challenge Cup semi-finals and 17 Lancashire Cup finals. In later years, the Championship final (and its successor the Premiership final) was staged at the ground, 9 such matches taking place between 1965 and 1980. Sadly, Station Road, showing signs of deterioration, fell out of favour in the 1980s, the last major game being the 1984 Challenge Cup semi-final between Leeds and Widnes.

The Lions, as Swinton are famously known, entertained their fans with two truly exceptional teams during their time at Station Road. The seeds of the first was already sown at Chorley Road in the 1920s, the second emerging in 1958/59 to thrill the crowds throughout much of the 1960s.

During the 1992 close season, the club's directors sold Station Road for property development, the team moving to Gigg Lane, home of Bury AFC, for 1992/93. In 2003, Swinton shared the ground of Salford City AFC at Moor Lane, Kersal, and, at the time of writing, are considering a further move, to the home of Sedgley Park RUFC in Whitefield for 2004.

The Swinton team in 1925/26. From left to right, standing: Harry Entwhistle, Fred Beswick, Bert Morris, Miller Strong, Henry Blewer, Tom Halliwell, Billy Price, Frank Evans. Seated: Jack Evans, Chris Brockbank, Hector Halsall (captain), Billo Rees, Albert Atkinson. The photograph was taken before the opening game of the season, a home win (20-10) over Rochdale Hornets on 29 August, a campaign that brought success in the Lancashire Cup and the Challenge Cup. They were the first triumphs in a glorious period that brought home four Championships, two Challenge Cups, two Lancashire Cups and four Lancashire League Championships over ten seasons.

Swinton players and officials in 1962/63, the season when the Lions regained the Championship after a twenty-eight-year gap, repeating the feat the following year. From left to right, standing: Cliff Evans (coach), Derek Clarke, Ken Roberts, Malcolm Cummings, Dick Bonser, John Speed, Alan Buckley, Harold Bate, Ron Morgan, Ken Halliwell, Vic Jones (secretary), Graham Rees. Seated: Peter Norburn, Bobby Fleet, Albert Blan (captain), William Scholes (chairman), John Stopford. Kneeling: Albert Cartwright, Graham Williams, George Parkinson, Ken Gowers, Trevor Roberts, Frank Halliwell.

Flying left wingman John Stopford scores one his two tries in the opening round of the Lancashire Cup, an 18-7 win over Warrington at Station Road in September 1961. His 42 touchdowns in 1963/64 is still a club record.

John Speed operated on the right flank in the Lions' exciting three-quarter line of that period. Here, his progress is checked by St Helens' Mick Sullivan during the 1961 Lancashire Cup final. The Saints' Ray French (the future BBC television commentator) looks on. Played at Wigan in front of 30,000 during November, St Helens won 25-9. Swinton reached four county finals in five years between 1960 and 1964, frustratingly losing to St Helens in each of them.

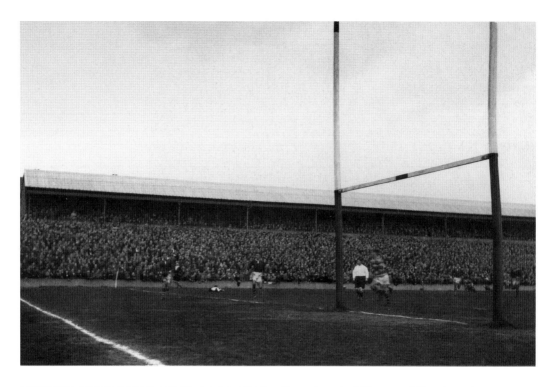

THE RUGBY FOOTBALL LEAGUE

Challenge Cup Semi-Final
—— RE-PLAY ——

BARROW v. LEIGH

WEDNESDAY
3rd APRIL
1957

At STATION ROAD
SWINTON

Kick-off 5.0 p.m.

OFFICIAL SOUVENIR PROGRAMME - Price 6d.

Above: A packed Townsend Road stand provides the background in this action shot from the 1948 Challenge Cup semi-final between Rochdale Hornets and Wigan at Station Road. An attendance of 26,004 saw Wigan win 11-0 on the way to recapturing the trophy at Wembley after a nineteen-year gap. Three years later, Wigan beat Warrington 3-2 in another semi-final, watched by Station Road's record attendance of 44,621.

Left: Swinton staged two Challenge Cup semi-final replays, the first being in 1957, when the great Barrow team of that era finally overcame Leigh 15-10 in front of 28,081 spectators, on the way to winning the cup at Wembley for the only time. The pair had originally fought out a nail-biting 2-2 draw at Wigan.

Above: The second Challenge Cup replay at Swinton was in 1964, but this was dramatically abandoned due to fading light in extra-time, Station Road – like most Rugby League grounds at that time – not having any floodlights. Oldham were leading Hull Kingston Rovers 17-14 but it was the Rovers who won the second replay at Huddersfield to reach their first Wembley final. Here, Hull Kingston Rovers stand-off Alan Burwell is on the way to going over the line for his side's opening try in the Station Road encounter, despite the attentions of Oldham's Trevor Sims (left) and Frank Dyson.

Right: The 1984 Challenge Cup semi-final was the last big match allocated to Station Road, a crowd of 14,046 seeing Widnes overcome Leeds 15-4.

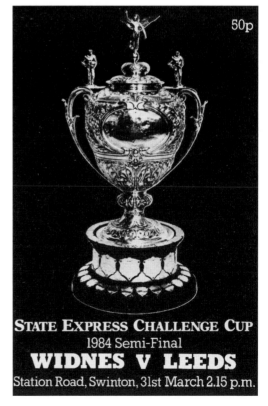

50p

STATE EXPRESS CHALLENGE CUP
1984 Semi-Final
WIDNES V LEEDS
Station Road, Swinton, 31st March 2.15 p.m.

Above: The Broughton Rangers team on 5 January 1935, before a home game with Wigan. Despite losing 18–8, the 'new look' Rangers were enjoying their best form for twenty years. From left to right, back row: Alf Scott (trainer), Ned Hodgson, Fred Smith, Bill Morgan, Joe Walsh, George Saddington, Trevor Thomas. Front row: Jack Garvey, Billy Stott, Tom Kenny, Ernie Thompson (captain), Jim Cumberbatch, Bryn Howells, Dai Thomas. Earlier in the season (on Saturday 20 October 1934), the Rangers had beaten Leigh 27–7 at Belle Vue in a match watched by the Duke of York. It was the first occasion that a member of the Royal Family had witnessed a Rugby League match in the provinces, the future King George VI arriving just before half-time, during which he met players and officials of both clubs plus Rugby Football League chairman Jim Lewthwaite and secretary John Wilson. He watched approximately 15 minutes of the second-half from the directors' box before continuing his tour. Earlier, he had witnessed the start of Manchester City's game with Derby County at Maine Road.

Opposite below left: The arrival of Jack Garvey from St Helens during the 1934 close season as the stand-off partner for Ernie Thompson was considered to be something of a coup for the Rangers. It was a collaboration that helped the club climb to sixth place in the League table for the 1935/36 campaign, although Garvey himself (in a January 1936 interview) admitted it took time to get a settled team and game-plan due to so many new players arriving after the move to Belle Vue. Garvey took over as club captain in 1936/37, but his stay was all too brief and he moved to Wigan midway through that season after appearing in just 79 matches. He played once each for England (partnering Thompson against Wales at Pontypridd in November 1936) and Lancashire whilst attached to the Rangers, having previously represented both during his St Helens days.

Opposite below right: Former Welsh Rugby Union international full-back Bryn Howells proved himself one of Rangers' best signings from the Valleys. Following his defection from Llanelli, he made his debut in January 1935, playing 152 matches for the club in a career effectively ended by the Second World War. He was described as 'a beautiful footballer' capable of catching any ball whilst being a good field-position kicker himself. He was particularly adept in the art of scoring drop-goals, contributing to his overall total of 217 goals and 446 points for the Rangers. Representative honours eluded him in Rugby League where he was constantly 'reserve' full-back for Wales, the legendary Wigan ace Jim Sullivan never missing a match!

CRYSTAL PALACE.

General Manager · · · Sir HENRY BUCKLAND

RUGBY LEAGUE FOOTBALL

STREATHAM & MITCHAM

versus

BROUGHTON RANGERS

AT THE

CRYSTAL PALACE

Saturday, May 11th, 1935

Kick Off 3.15 p.m.

ADMISSION:—

Ground **1/-** Boys **6d.** Pavilion 1/- extra
Stands 6d. extra.

2d. Official Programme **2d.**

H. D. JACKSON, Printer, &c. &c.

Above left: The programme cover for Broughton Rangers' match at Crystal Palace in May 1935. Although the opposition was labelled 'Streatham & Mitcham', they met a side that would form the nucleus of both that club and Acton & Willesden, the London duo entering teams for the 1935/36 season. The Palace was utilised because the newcomers' grounds were still being prepared. On a beautiful day, the Rangers won 17-13 in front of what was described as a moderate attendance. The local paper suggested the low turnout was because people were following 'more seasonal pursuits' but, on a positive note, added that 'more of the ball was seen on Saturday, than would have been seen in any Rugby Union game'. Despite such an upbeat view of the thirteen-a-side code, both clubs folded within two years.

Above right: Tom Spedding's name dominates the twenty-two years that the Rangers were at Belle Vue after taking on the role of supporter's club secretary when Rugby League first moved there. He was born in the vicinity and previously spent fourteen years as the Physical Education and Sports Secretary for the Lancashire & Cheshire Division of the YMCA. He was also a licensed Master of Ceremonies for the British Boxing Board of Control. A *Rugby League Gazette* feature (in February 1948) recalled: 'At their new (Belle Vue) headquarters they (Rangers) were in the midst of a soccer-minded public, and no one realised this more than (Broughton Rangers) secretary Jack Hoey, who was more than pleased to find a really enthusiastic helper in Tom Spedding, who was in charge of the Supporters Club. Inside two years, Hoey had resigned and, in his place, their present secretary-manager (Spedding) took the helm.' Following the Second World War, Spedding was particularly instrumental in keeping the club alive.

In 1936, the Ardath Tobacco Company of London issued 'Photocards' featuring rugby and soccer teams. The sets were regionalised – a 'Lancashire' series of 110 cards including two of Broughton Rangers: the first and 'A' (reserve) team. Above is the one featuring Rangers' first team, from left to right, back row (standing): Captain Stuart Hampson (director), Dr J. Wishart (director), Ted Smith (trainer), W. Barnes, George Mills, Dick Manning, Bert Cambridge, Frank Whitcombe, Bill Morgan, Alf Scott (masseur), Bert Atkinson (director), George Wilson (vice-chairman). Seated: Bryn Howells, George Bunter, Jack Garvey (captain), Jim Cumberbatch, Glyn Jones, Billy Stott. On ground (surrounded by ball boys): Tom Kenny, Ernie Thompson. The photograph was probably taken before the match against Keighley (won 36-0) on 2 May 1936 at Belle Vue. The final 1935/36 League placing of sixth was the highest achieved whilst at Belle Vue. The players are in the blue-and-white quartered jerseys introduced that season, and retained until 1946.

The Rangers 'A' team was the only Rugby League second-string side featured in the Ardath set due to their success of winning the Rugby League Combination Championship and Lancashire Combination Championship in 1935/36, both for the first time. The trophy shown is for the former competition (open to all reserve sides) and originally provided by the Rugby League authorities for the short-lived Welsh League that existed for three seasons from 1908/09. From left to right, back row: Tom Spedding (secretary), Billy Doran, Dai Thomas, Wilf Sulway, Wilf Foster, Walter Brown, Fred Smith, Bill Morgan, Jack Beetham, F. Davies (trainer). Front row: W. Brydon, Joe Luckey, F. Hillman, Tommy Blinkhorn (captain), J. McPhail, Wilf Selby, Dai Davies, Billy McGarrigan. Despite this success, the Rangers entered their reserves in the Manchester & District League from 1937/38 (until the Second World War) as amateurs in a cost-cutting exercise.

Above left: The team sheet for the Rangers' public practice match at Belle Vue stadium on
22 August 1936. The 'Blue & White Quarters' – the probable first team captained by Jack Garvey
– defeated the 'Stripes', led by Tommy Blinkhorn, 25-16. Public practice (or trial) matches were a
regular pre-season feature for all Rugby League clubs at one time and usually took place the
weekend before the first match, featuring first-choice and reserve players, plus a few hopefuls.
These games were often the first time that future heroes were seen in action by supporters.

Above right: A poster advertising the opening match of the 1936/37 season against Warrington,
which the Rangers won 10-7. Supporters are also encouraged to buy their season tickets with the
most expensive touted as one guinea.

Below left: The teams for the Broughton Rangers *v.* Newcastle fixture in November 1937 (won 35-5 by Rangers) include Jim Cumberbatch on the Tynesiders' wing. Cumberbatch was having his second outing after leaving Broughton a few weeks earlier. Although he won his second England cap against Wales the following January, it was an ill-fated move for Cumberbatch as Newcastle folded at the season's end after just two years in existence. A report in January 1939 claimed the Rangers had had to sell Cumberbatch and Salford-bound prop-forward Bert Cambridge 'to save the club's finances'. A further report the following month suggested 'Rangers may not continue next season' the club dismissing this as nothing more than an inaccurate rumour.

Below right: Broughton Rangers, under the captaincy of Ernie Thompson, met an Australian touring side for the sixth time on Christmas Day 1937. It was certainly a 'Merry Christmas' for the 3,000 supporters (the Rangers' lowest attendance for a match against a touring team) as they won 13-0. This, and a 14-12 victory in 1909, was the club's only success against the Australians.

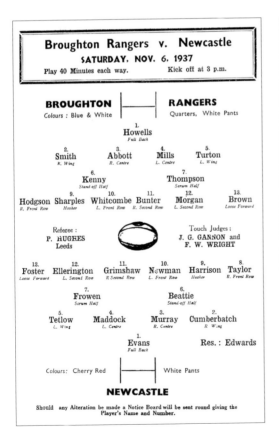

THE SCRUM

The Magazine Programme

OF THE

BROUGHTON RANGERS

BELLE VUE LIMITED

RUGBY FOOTBALL CLUB

No. 16.   SATURDAY, APRIL 9th, 1938   Twopence

RUGBY LEAGUE CHALLENGE CUP

SEMI-FINAL

SALFORD

versus

SWINTON

Played at Belle Vue, Manchester.   Kick Off 3-30

FOWLER'S "A.I." PIES

ARE PERFECT   SOLD AT ALL BARS ON BELLE VUE GROUND

The second highest crowd to attend a Rugby League match at Belle Vue (after the 1933 Test Match) is 31,664 for the 1938 Rugby League Challenge Cup semi-final between Salford and Swinton. It is probable, however, that the attendance went closer to 40,000, many climbing in as chaos reigned outside the stadium as throngs of supporters descended upon the turnstiles, the gates being closed before the start to all but ticket holders. A few minutes before play started, a handful of fans clambered over the barrier on to the speedway track, a move that encouraged hundreds more around the stadium to follow suit, completely enveloping the playing area in a repeat of the scenes at the Test Match. During the game players found themselves colliding with spectators, who were stood six or seven deep around the touchline. The tie finished 6-0 in Salford's favour, the 'Red Devils' going on to achieve their only Wembley victory.

THE SCRUM

The Magazine Programme

OF THE

BROUGHTON RANGERS

BELLE VUE LIMITED

RUGBY FOOTBALL CLUB

No. 7.   NOVEMBER 12th, 1938   Twopence

Next Rugby League Match

ON THIS STADIUM

Saturday, November 26th

Broughton Rangers

versus

ST. HELENS

Kick-off 2-45 p.m.

The Boughton Rangers *Magazine Programme* for the 1938/39 season could, at first glance, have confused supporters into thinking they were at the wrong match! This particular game on 12 November saw the Rangers entertain Halifax (losing 18-10). The St Helens fixture, so prominently advertised on the front cover, was, in fact, a fortnight away.

FOWLER'S "A.I." PIES

ARE PERFECT   SOLD AT ALL BARS ON BELLE VUE GROUND

17/19, DAWSON STREET, MANCHESTER 3.   TELEPHONE BLA. 7645

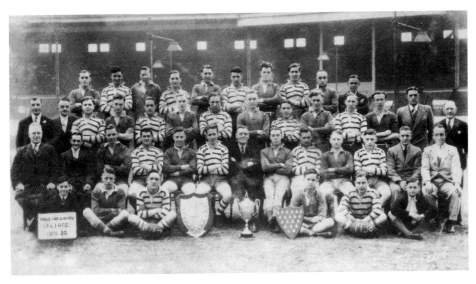

Several years in advance of the Rangers adopting the name of Belle Vue in their title, the Belle Vue Juniors team (for players under twenty-one) played at Greenbank Fields on Manor Road, Levenshulme. In 1938/39 they swept all before them, winning the Salford Continuation League and Salford Challenge Cup. This postcard commemorates their success, the full squad assembling inside the speedway stadium to show off their prized silverware.

BROUGHTON RANGERS

BELLE VUE LIMITED

RUGBY FOOTBALL CLUB

President   -   -   -   -   -   GEORGE WILSON
Directors : George Wilson, B. L. Atkinson, Dr. J. Wishart, Captain S. H. Hampson, M.C., J.P., J. Whalen, J.P., C. Batty
Hon. Secretary   -   -   -   -   -   TOM SPEDDING

OFFICIAL PROGRAMME   -   -   ONE PENNY

Saturday, 18th May, 1940   Kick-off 3-30

LANCASHIRE R.L. SUMMER CUP COMPETITION

BROUGHTON RANGERS v. SALFORD

Although Belle Vue was the only speedway track in Britain operating throughout the Second World War, Broughton Rangers had to vacate the stadium, the field being occupied by the military. After several 'home' matches on opponents' grounds, a meeting with Stockport County AFC in February 1940 resulted in Rangers having use of their Edgeley Park enclosure. The first match, a Lancashire Cup tie with St Helens on 9 March, drew 4,000 people despite heavy rain, the Rangers' goal posts from Belle Vue being used. Two months later (as illustrated by this programme cover) they entertained Salford at Stockport in a short-lived Summer League competition, losing 65-15, the biggest 'home' defeat in Rangers' history. Like many, Broughton struggled to complete their fixtures and, following a match at Edgeley Park on 18 October 1941 (which had an attendance of only 200), they suspended activities until peace returned. Of 25 home fixtures played during hostilities, 10 were at Stockport, the rest on opposition territory.

Above: Broughton Rangers' third home fixture following the war was against Hull Kingston Rovers on 15 September 1945. A Rangers player, surrounded by Rovers defenders (wearing that club's traditional white jersey and red band) scores by the goal posts, one of six tries in a 32-13 win. After the pre-war gossip forecasting the club's demise, it was encouraging to see the stands looking full on their return to action.

Right: The Broughton Rangers programme cover prophetically proclaims them 'The Belle Vue Team' and just under two months later – at Hull Kingston Rovers on 11 May 1946 – the Rangers would play their final game as 'Broughton', emerging with the name of their adopted home the following season. This cover also announced a short tour of France was to be undertaken, the Rangers defeating Perpignan 18-14 on Saturday 30 March 1946 and losing 26-12 to Carcassonne the following day. Club officials said they were given an overwhelming reception adding: 'Everywhere we have been feted and cheered as friends and sportsmen. Our presentation of the silver caskets to the teams of Perpignan and Carcassonne, the planting of the soil of England in the soil of France, has undoubtedly created a precedent in the annals of Rugby Football History.'

We have accepted an invitation extended to us from the Rugby League, to play two matches in the South of France, on Saturday, March 30th and Sunday, March 31st. In consequence of this the Leeds Home Match for March 30th will be re-arranged.

The Matches to be played in the South of France will be respectively at Perpignan and Carcassonne. Arrangements are well in hand and the Team will leave Manchester on Monday, March 25th and return to England the early part of the following week.

Swinton are to visit us to-day and as we beat them last Saturday on the Swinton ground, no doubt they will be "all out" to level matters by attempting to take the points away from Belle-Vue this afternoon. Whatever may be the result, we hope that both teams will play football that will satisfy the supporters of both Clubs present this afternoon.

BROUGHTON RANGERS
RUGBY FOOTBALL CLUB
BELLE VUE, MANCHESTER

SWINTON v. BROUGHTON RANGERS
The Belle Vue Team

Saturday, March 16th, 1946 — Kick-off 3-30

OFFICIAL PROGRAMME   -   -   -   TWOPENCE

eight

Maine Road

Manchester City AFC's former Maine Road enclosure in Moss Side opened in August 1923. The club had moved from their previous Hyde Road ground (approximately one mile from the Belle Vue complex and their home since 1887) because the 40,000 capacity was insufficient for their growing number of fans. In the early 1920s, City had considered leasing land at Belle Vue (the same site the speedway stadium would later be built on), deciding it was not large enough and voting for Moss Side instead.

The record attendance at Maine Road is 84,569 for a 1934 Manchester City v. Stoke City FA Cup match, the capacity being reduced considerably in later years. Manchester United shared the stadium after Old Trafford was blitzed during the Second World War in March 1941, staying until the end of the 1948/49 campaign. With Maine Road having floodlighting from 1953 (four years before Old Trafford) United continued to use the ground for mid-week games, most notably the start of their European quest in 1956.

With interest in the Rugby League Championship final growing (54,000 saw the 1938 final at Leeds United AFC's Elland Road ground), a larger venue was required. Maine Road (with goal posts borrowed from Broughton Rangers' Belle Vue ground) was used for the first time in May 1939, Castleford and Salford attracting a British Rugby League record attendance. With crowds often in excess of 60,000, Maine Road continued to provide the setting for all peacetime finals until 1956, excepting the 1952 decider in Huddersfield.

Over thirty years later, on consecutive days in January 1987, the thirteen-a-side game returned to Maine Road. Oldham (versus Featherstone Rovers, attendance 2,719) and Warrington (against Barrow, 2,215) hiring the ground for League fixtures, taking advantage of the under-soil heating when their own pitches had frozen over. In 1989, the Warrington v. Wigan Challenge Cup semi-final was taken to Maine Road, the only time a match in that competition was held there.

That was the last time competitive Rugby League took place at the stadium. The word 'competitive' is deliberate as the only game since was the so-called 'Cross Code' match on the evening of 8 May 1996, Wigan meeting Bath Rugby Union club under Rugby League rules, the attendance being 20,148.

When Manchester City announced its move to the City of Manchester Stadium for the 2003/04 soccer season, it was anticipated that Sale Sharks Rugby Union club (whose Heywood Road ground has a 5,786 capacity) would transfer to Maine Road, Manchester City Council reportedly offering to invest £2.5m to redevelop it into a 17,000 all-seated venue. In March 2003, however, it was stated negotiations had fallen through and that the stadium would be demolished, Sale subsequently unveiling plans to share Stockport County's Edgeley Park from 2003/04.

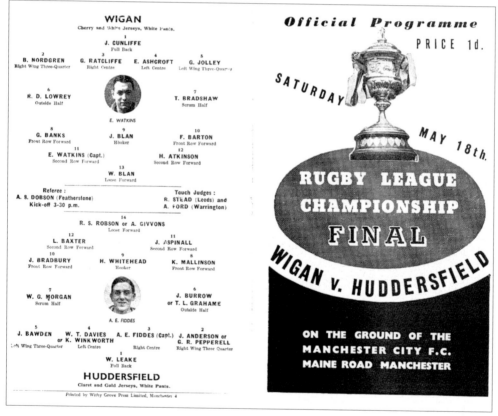

WIGAN
Cherry and White Jerseys, White Pants.

1
J. CUNLIFFE
Full Back

2
B. NORDGREN
Right Wing Three-Quarter

3
G. RATCLIFFE
Right Centre

4
E. ASHCROFT
Left Centre

5
G. JOLLEY
Left Wing Three-Quarter

6
R. D. LOWREY
Outside Half

7
T. BRADSHAW
Scrum Half

E. WATKINS

8
G. BANKS
Front Row Forward

9
J. BLAN
Hooker

10
F. BARTON
Front Row Forward

11
E. WATKINS (Capt.)
Second Row Forward

12
H. ATKINSON
Second Row Forward

13
W. BLAN
Loose Forward

Referee :
A. S. DOBSON (Featherstone)
Kick-off 3-30 p.m.

Touch Judges :
R. STEAD (Leeds) and
A. FORD (Warrington)

14
R. S. ROBSON or A. GIVVONS
Loose Forward

12
L. BAXTER
Second Row Forward

11
J. ASPINALL
Second Row Forward

10
J. BRADBURY
Front Row Forward

9
H. WHITEHEAD
Hooker

8
K. MALLINSON
Front Row Forward

7
W. G. MORGAN
Scrum Half

6
J. BURROW
or T. L. GRAHAME
Outside Half

A. E. FIDDES

5
J. BAWDEN
Left Wing Three-Quarter

4
W. T. DAVIES
or K. WINKWORTH
Left Centre

3
A. E. FIDDES (Capt.)
Right Centre

2
**J. ANDERSON or
G. R. PEPPERELL**
Right Wing Three Quarter

1
W. LEAKE
Full Back

HUDDERSFIELD
Claret and Gold Jerseys, White Pants.

Printed by Withy Grove Press Limited, Manchester 4

Official Programme

PRICE 1d.

SATURDAY

MAY 18th.

**RUGBY LEAGUE
CHAMPIONSHIP
FINAL**

WIGAN v. HUDDERSFIELD

**ON THE GROUND OF THE
MANCHESTER CITY F.C.
MAINE ROAD MANCHESTER**

Above: With peace restored, the Rugby League hierarchy wasted no time in returning to Maine Road for the 1946 final, Wigan being crowned as the first post-Second World War champions by defeating Huddersfield 13-4. It was widely anticipated that the attendance would exceed that for 1939 but, in the event, it fell just short at 67,136. Shown here is the outer cover of the single sheet programme – paper being in short supply after the war.

Opposite above: Action from the Castleford *v.* Salford 1939 Championship final, the first Rugby League game played at Maine Road. This newspaper photograph, published in the *Leeds Mercury*, shows Salford's stand-off Tom Kenny (the former Broughton Rangers player) about to evade Castleford loose-forward Fred Brindle (on left) on the way to scoring his side's first try in an 8-6 victory. The 69,504 attendance was the biggest so far for a Rugby League match in Great Britain, guaranteeing its place as the number one choice for future finals.

Right: Wigan returned to Maine Road in 1947 to face Dewsbury, who were appearing in their first peacetime Championship final. Due to a severe winter, which caused mass postponements to the fixture list, the final did not take place until 21 June, some five weeks later than scheduled.

Below: Action from the 1947 Championship final as a scrum breaks up with Dewsbury (left) in possession. Wigan retained the title, repeating their 13-4 scoreline of the previous final.

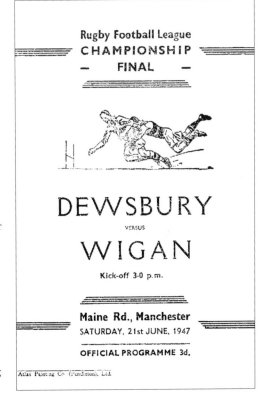

Rugby Football League
CHAMPIONSHIP
— FINAL —

DEWSBURY

VERSUS

WIGAN

Kick-off 3-0 p.m.

Maine Rd., Manchester
SATURDAY, 21st JUNE, 1947

OFFICIAL PROGRAMME 3d.

Atlas Printing Co (Pendleton), Ltd.

When Huddersfield took on reigning champions, Warrington, in the 1949 decider it filled Maine Road to the rafters, drawing a record Championship final crowd of 75,194 (a figure subsequently bettered only once, by the 83,190 who saw the Wakefield *v.* Wigan 1960 final at Odsal Stadium, Bradford). They were not disappointed as the match had an exciting finish, Warrington storming back from a 13-point deficit to just miss out 13-12. Here, Huddersfield scrum-half Billy Banks is about to pass to Russ Pepperell (number 6).

Huddersfield returned the following year to defend their title, opposing Wigan in a repeat of the 1946 Maine Road final. The 1950 British tourists had already set sail for Australia, taking eight of Wigan's leading players (none from Huddersfield), ensuring the pre-match odds favoured the Yorkshire side. Here, we see Huddersfield's Aussie full-back John Hunter (with the ball) attempting to break out of his own half by 'handing off' Wigan centre Jack Broome (in hoops).

Above: Nat Silcock's sensational try for Wigan after only two minutes of the 1950 Championship final put his team on course for a 20-2 victory over Huddersfield. The match was dubbed Wigan's 'finest hour'.

Left: In 1955, Warrington met Oldham in the penultimate Championship decider to be staged at Maine Road. Heavy rain created poor playing conditions, the scoring coming late as Warrington narrowly won 7-3 to retain the trophy, having beaten Halifax at Maine Road the previous year. It was Warrington's third success on the ground, their total of five Championship final appearances in this period being the most by any club at Moss Side. Following the 1956 Halifax *v.* Hull final, the event transferred to Bradford's Odsal Stadium.

In 1989, Maine Road was the venue for the Challenge Cup semi-final between Warrington and Wigan. Wigan won the match 13-6 to set up a return to Wembley during a period of domination that saw them succeed at the Twin Towers for eight consecutive years. Particularly noteworthy was Joe Lydon's late long-range drop-goal when Warrington and Wigan were level at 6-6. Measured as covering 61yds, it is thought to be a record for the sport in Britain.

The Rugby Football League
SILK CUT CHALLENGE CUP

1988/89 SEMI-FINAL
WARRINGTON v WIGAN
MAINE ROAD, MANCHESTER
MARCH 25th 1989 3.15pm
PRICE 80p

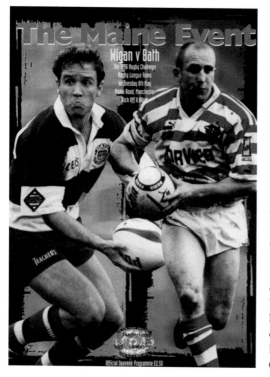

When the Rugby Football Union declared itself to be a professional sport in 1995, it opened the way for Wigan to meet the Bath Rugby Union club in two 'Cross Code' challenge matches. The first, played under Rugby League rules, was held at Maine Road, the programme cover featuring rival captains Phil de Glanville of Bath (left) and Wigan's Shaun Edwards. Wigan led 52-0 at half-time on the way to their 82-6 victory over the West Country side, former Rosslyn Park RU wing, Martin Offiah registering 6 of his side's 16 tries.

nine

Belle Vue Rangers

Following a survey of supporters' views in 1938, a Rangers official commented: 'The most impressive feature of the replies is that they have all come from the new area. Not even a postcard has arrived from Broughton, which I consider rather significant.' The Broughton Rangers name finally disappeared in 1946, replaced by the more appropriate title of Belle Vue Rangers. Broughton Rangers Supporters' Club, who met at the Griffin Hotel, Broughton, continued organising trips to games and raising funds but interest waned after the change and they disbanded in 1949, the £10 in their account being presented to the Gorton-based Belle Vue Supporters' Club.

Attendances declined after the initial post-war crowd boom, although Tom Spedding, now a director, secretary and team manager, was still 'acquiring good players on limited funding'. In 1947, officials denied they planned to discard players and said they were 'concentrating on making further additions'. Rumours, in January 1949, that the club was leaving Belle Vue received a very strong denial by the club directors. Nonetheless, international wing Stan McCormick transferred that month to St Helens for £4,000, one writer claiming although it 'staved off the shutdown it only delayed the inevitable'. McCormick, years later, reflected: 'It was £5 winning money and we weren't always sure of getting that. Sometimes they'd ask us to leave it over while they got some more money in the kitty.'

At the RFL Management Committee meeting on 20 April 1955, a letter was read from Belle Vue Gardens Ltd complaining that Rangers had not paid £600 rent for 1954/55. In May, it was revealed the club actually owed creditors £1,600 (including the rent). The committee agreed to guarantee the rent for 1955/56 (as they had in 1953/54), but on 18 June, it was reported Belle Vue Gardens had refused further use of the stadium. The club requested permission to revert to the Broughton Rangers title, intending to play at Fallowfield Stadium. The committee agreed provided four conditions were met. On 9 August, however, the following press report was issued:

'The Management Committee ... very much regret that they cannot see that it is possible for the Club to fulfil their League fixtures this coming season as they have not complied with the conditions laid down ... which were as follows:
(a) Provide a suitable ground at a reasonable rental.
(b) Provide a properly constituted club and committee.
(c) Provide a list of registered players.
(d) Provide adequate financial backing.'

Belle Vue Stadium closed following a stock car meeting on 14 November 1987, speedway finishing on 1 November, the promoter of both (since 1982) Stuart Bamforth, having purchased the stadium from Trust House Forte, selling the site. It is now occupied by ADT Car Auctions, with speedway returning to the greyhound stadium.

Above: A new beginning. The Belle Vue Rangers team on 31 August 1946, before their first match under that name (a 12-11 home defeat against Wigan). The name change was marked with a return to blue and white hooped jerseys. The club continued to wear white shorts – the subtle change from black having taken place following the move to Belle Vue Stadium in 1933. From left to right, back row: Tommy Tolan, Mel Tierney, Tom Kenny, Jack Waring, Dai Thomas, Dick Manning, Walter Brown. Seated: Albert Harris, Glyn Jones (captain), Stan McCormick, Elwyn Gwyther. On ground: John Clinton, Billy Watkins. Northumbrian-born Kenny, who made 248 appearances with Rangers, had rejoined the club from Dewsbury, having transferred to Salford in 1938.

Opposite below: Dai Thomas, like Glyn Jones, joined the Rangers from Swansea in September 1933. He played in 150 matches for the club, 99 of them in his final three seasons (1945/46 to 1947/48) when, at prop-forward, he established himself as 'a sound scrummager', taking his place in the Lancashire Cup final teams of 1946 and 1947. During the 1948/49 season he shared a testimonial with pack-mates Walter Brown, Jones and Dick Manning. His final first-team match for the Rangers was in January 1948.

Above left: Hooker Glyn Jones had been one of the Rangers' first acquisitions after they moved to Belle Vue, joining the club in September 1933 from Swansea Rugby Union club. It was, therefore, appropriate that he should be the first captain of the re-titled Belle Vue Rangers, leading the side in the 1946 Lancashire Cup final. His lengthy Rangers career did not conclude until January 1951, after 291 appearances. His only representative honour was during March 1946 when he played for his native Wales against France in Bordeaux.

Above right: Second-row forward Walter Brown was a local signing from Pendlebury Juniors, making his debut for the Rangers in 1932. He was destined to play 160 times for the club, his career – like so many – being disrupted by the Second World War. Brown was a member of the Belle Vue Rangers team that appeared in the 1946 Lancashire Cup final against Wigan, his final match being in October 1949.

Action at Belle Vue Stadium as the ball goes loose during a Rangers *v.* Liverpool Stanley Lancashire Cup first-round tie on 14 September 1946. The two players on their hands and knees in the foreground are Stanley prop Riley (number 10) and Rangers' second-row Tommy Tolan (12, in hoops). In what was the club's third match as Belle Vue Rangers, they won 11-5 on their way to reaching the final.

Full-back Melbourne 'Mel' Tierney signed for the Rangers from Tumble Rugby Union club of South Wales in August 1946, following a trial. Competition for the full-back jersey increased with the arrival of Albert Gregory in 1948, and Tierney moved to the centre before establishing himself in the second row during 1949, a role he fulfilled until the club folded in 1955. His consistent form is evident through his club record of 137 consecutive appearances from September 1950 until December 1953. This Belle Vue publicity shot shows him taking a kick at goal although, in fact, he only did this on an irregular basis for the club. He was, however, the Rangers' leading marksman in 1951/52 (51 goals) and 1953/54 (59), notching 145 in 311 outings. He was at centre in the 1947 Lancashire Cup final, having been unfit for the previous year's final. He played twice in the pack for Wales, the second time – against France 'B' on 19 May 1955 in Nantes – was significant as it was to be the last appearance by a Rangers player in a match, the club disbanding shortly after. He was also Belle Vue captain in their final 1954/55 season.

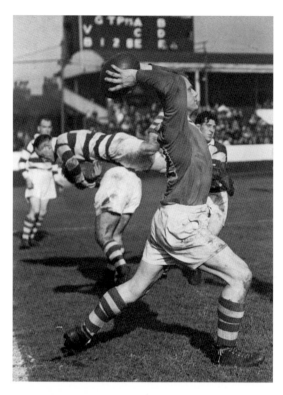

Left: Salford forward Jack Brown attempts an unorthodox pass at Belle Vue on 28 September 1946. Belle Vue were, according to the scoreboard in the background, 8-0 ahead at this stage and they eventually won 13-5. Brown, who had guested for Rangers on one occasion during the Second World War, moved to Huddersfield before following the example of elder brother, Walter, by joining the club in September 1954. He subsequently extended his appearance total for Rangers to 29, including the club's last match – at Workington Town on 5 May 1955.

Below: Another action shot from the Belle Vue Rangers *v.* Salford match in September 1946, as full-back Mel Tierney just manages to push the visitors' loose-forward Dai Moses into touch, preventing a certain try. As the packed stand testifies, the traditional rivals attracted a sizeable crowd at the time, 15,000 watching on this occasion.

Rangers winger Ted Cope halts an Australian attack watched by colleague Doug Phillips (on extreme left).

Belle Vue prop Elwyn Gwyther bursts through a gap against the Australians in 1948.

Above left: Wigan-born full-back Albert Gregory was signed from Warrington in 1948. A sound, dependable defender, he was also a reliable marksman, holding two club records for his prowess with the boot: most career goals (308 from 214 appearances) and most in a single season (86 in 1950/51). He is also second in the Rangers all-time points table with 655. He spent seven campaigns with Belle Vue Rangers, including the club's final 1954/55 season. He had two younger brothers, Arthur and Harold, who played for Salford.

Above right: A Belle Vue programme cover for the 1948/49 season. The game in question is a League match against Barrow in April, which the Rangers won 8-2. It was an unexpected result as Barrow finished fourth to qualify for the Championship play-off, whereas the Rangers were down at twenty-first – their lowest finish since 1933/34. The upcoming marriage of Eric Ayles, referred to in the programme notes, was to Albert Gregory's sister.

Opposite below: These caricatures of Belle Vue Rangers personalities appeared in the *Manchester Evening News* during March 1951. The 1950/51 campaign was the club's best post-war season, finishing twelfth in the League. The strength of the team, brilliantly led by halves Ray Price and Dai Rees (who made 222 appearances for the Rangers after transferring from Oldham in August 1948), lay in the pack. As can be seen from the illustration here, the majority of the side was Welsh and Phillips' full name – as implied by the caption – really was Douglas Versailles Phillips!

Above: A postcard of the Rangers for 1948/49, featuring the team at Belle Vue before the opening match of the season against Workington Town on 21 August (lost 12-2). From left to right, back row: Eric Ayles, Mel Tierney, Bryn Day, Jack Fearnley, Elwyn Gwyther, Bill Flanagan, Harry Pimblett. Seated: Doug Phillips, Dai Rees, Ted Cope, Stan McCormick (captain), Ray Price, A. Ogden.

Above: The Belle Vue Rangers team on 15 October 1951 at Wigan before losing 22-9 to the home side in a Lancashire Cup semifinal. From left to right, back row: Eric Ayles, Harry Pimblett, John Norburn, Dai Bevan, Bill Hunt, Mel Tierney, Dai Morgan. Front row: Ray Price, Ken Ogden, Elwyn Gwyther, Doug Phillips (captain), Albert Gregory, Dai Rees. Winger Bevan was signed in December 1948 from Oldham RU, although originating from Tonypandy. He scored 49 tries in 131 matches before moving to Wigan in 1952, where he earned caps for Great Britain and Wales. He transferred to Halifax in 1953, appearing at Wembley in 1954. Morgan, another Welsh recruit, arrived from Huddersfield in September 1948, the centre making 243 Belle Vue appearances before joining Swinton after the club's demise in 1955.

Left: The match against the 1951 New Zealanders was the last time the Rangers met a touring side. A try from Elwyn Gwyther and two goals by Mel Tierney secured a narrow 7-5 win, the club's only success against the Kiwis in four meetings from 1907.

Above: Belle Vue Rangers photographed at their Hyde Road ground before a match on 21 February 1953. The visitors (for a League fixture) were eventual champions St Helens, who won 20-7. From left to right, back row: Eric Ayles, Mel Tierney, Jack Tonge, M. Gallagher, Harry Dagnan, Bill Hunt, George Beatty. Seated: Dai Morgan, Derek Day, Harry Pimblett (captain), Jack Mannion. Kneeling: Dai Rees, Albert Gregory. Skipper Pimblett, signed from Warrington in 1947, served the Rangers well, mostly in the three-quarter line, appearing in 271 matches over eight seasons. Beatty, a former New Zealand RU 'All Black', switched codes to join Leigh in 1950. He transferred to Belle Vue in January 1952 but, although tried in several back positions, was unable to establish himself, returning to New Zealand in 1954 after 28 matches.

Right: The 1954/55 campaign is drawing rapidly to a close and so is the life of the Rangers. This match at Belle Vue was the last time these two old adversaries would meet, Oldham winning 34-8 on the way to ending the League season in second place. The Rangers, conversely, finished second from last (in thirtieth position), their worst showing since 1927/28.

BELLE VUE RANGERS

Belle Vue Rangers (Broughton Rangers [Belle Vue] Limited)

Telephone : EASt 1331

Directors : Alderman W. H. Oldfield, J.P., M.P., J. Kay, T. Spedding and E. S. Davis
Secretary-Manager: T. Spedding   Hon. Club Physician: Dr. L. Loughran

versus

OLDHAM

SATURDAY, MARCH 12th, 1955. **Kick-off 3 p.m.**

OFFICIAL PROGRAMME - - *PRICE* 2d.

Above: A postcard, sent by the club's secretary-manager, Tom Spedding, to second-row forward John Hampton, advising him of his selection for the Belle Vue team, at home to Whitehaven on 26 March 1955. Hampton was one of two amateurs (the other was full-back Derek Hardman) who assisted the club in the latter stages of a financially difficult season. He played 6 times in the final months, including what was destined to be the Rangers' last match, at Workington on 5 May. The team's final appearance at Belle Vue was on 18 April against Salford, the lease at the stadium being terminated in June.

Left: Another interesting postcard from Tom Spedding to John Hampton which indicates, as late as 5 August 1955, that the Rangers anticipated starting the new season. The card invites Hampton for pre-season training 'on Monday next, 8th August 55 at the MAC (Manchester Athletic Club) Ground, Fallowfield, now known as the Harris Stadium'. Tuesday 9 August, however, was, to quote one journalist, 'an historic day, for it marked the end of Broughton Rangers', the RFL announcing their decision to remove the club from the 1955/56 fixtures. Apart from Fallowfield, Spedding made abortive requests to Salford, Swinton and Oldham, to share their grounds in place of their 'A' teams. Tom Bergin of the *Salford City Reporter*, lamented: 'It is difficult for an outsider to get the full picture. Most feel the Rugby League have failed dismally.' Spedding said he hoped to arrange friendly games at Fallowfield during the coming season and return in 1956/57, but it was not to be. After a history going back over seventy-eight years, the Rangers no longer existed.

ten

White City Stadium

White City Stadium was on Chester Road, a proverbial stone's throw from, and midway between, the famous Old Trafford venues of Manchester United and Lancashire County Cricket club. Built as a 40,000-capacity greyhound stadium and opening on Whit Monday, 28 May 1928, it was soon adapted for the new craze of dirt-track (speedway) racing. A quarter-mile circuit was laid inside the greyhound track, racing commencing on 16 June 1928 and continuing until 1930, at which point the Greyhound Racing Association took over the stadium, which then concentrated on canine activities.

Over the years, several diverse events have taken place at White City. Local athletic meetings were held from the early 1930s and, following the introduction of a six-lane cinder running track in 1953, many of the world's greatest athletes (including Derek Ibbotson, Paavo Nurmi, Gordon Pirie and Emil Zatopek) all ran there during the 1950s.

During the 1960s, the stadium was used by Salford Central AFC and, in 1967, it was Rugby Union's turn when the New Zealand All Blacks took on and defeated the North of England 33-3. In 1972, stock car racing came to White City, meetings continuing throughout the 1970s including the World Finals of 1976 and 1979.

Rugby League's White City moment came with the appearance of the 1961 New Zealanders during September. When White City was first announced as the venue for a tour match, the news was not well received by Salford and Swinton, who were both suspicious that it was being played with a view to establishing a club there.

Rumours of setting up another Manchester team had persisted since Belle Vue Rangers disbanded in 1955 (although, strictly speaking, White City was located in the nearby borough of Trafford), and both clubs were concerned about the possible affect on their attendances.

Certainly, the idea of selecting a Rugby League XIII to oppose the Kiwis presented an attractive fixture opportunity. It was a rare chance for some of the sport's most famous overseas 'imports' (whose Rugby League careers took place almost entirely in England) to play representative rugby against a touring side. After the match, it was stated that the attendance of 5,271 was 'encouraging to those who hoped to see a Rugby League club established there' although, in truth, it was the second lowest turnout of the tour.

In December 1961, the possibility of a White City team resurfaced when it was reported the stadium owners 'are to dispense with the athletics track and would be prepared to stage Rugby League', although the idea did not mature into reality.

White City closed its doors for the last time after the final greyhound meeting in October 1981, the site lying derelict for almost ten years before being sold and redeveloped as a retail park.

114

Opposite above: The gateway into White City, illustrated by this 1907 postcard. The famous white archway pre-dated the stadium by some years, being built as the entrance to the botanical gardens and zoo that opened there in 1827. When interest declined, the site was reopened in May 1907 as the White City Amusement Park, complete with a lake, attracting 32,972 visitors on the opening day. When the stadium replaced the amusement park, the archway was retained as its main entrance. Today, with the exception of the statues that stood at the top, it provides a landmark for the White City Retail Park, being a Grade II listed structure.

Right: The attractive-looking tour fixture between the Rugby League XIII and New Zealand, played on a Wednesday evening, had the additional novelty value of being under the gaze of the White City floodlights. At the time, only Leigh amongst the West Pennine Rugby League clubs possessed such a facility.

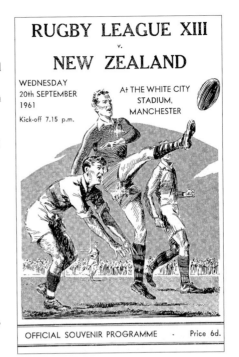

Above: The 1961 New Zealand touring party, led by captain Roger Hammond (seated centre of the middle row), flanked by tour manager Colin Riddle (left) and coach Bill Telford (in the official blazers). The match at White City came at the halfway point of their 20-match tour in which they managed to win just 8, losing the Test series 2-1.

Opposite below: White City Stadium in 1929 when speedway and greyhound racing was the regular diet for patrons. This aerial view shows Chester Road running past the far side of the stadium, the rear of the famous white archway protruding on the right of the main covered stand.

Right: The 5,271 curious spectators that made the journey to White City were rewarded with an entertaining game, the Rugby League XIII winning a closely fought encounter 22-20, the New Zealanders coming back strongly in the latter stages from a 20-5 deficit. Each team scored four tries, Brian Bevan (two), Alan Skene and Laurie Gilfedder crossing for the victors, with Fred Griffiths' five goals ultimately making a difference against the four from the boot of New Zealand full-back John Fagan.

Below: The Rugby League XIII line-up had a cosmopolitan look, led by South African full-back Fred Griffiths and containing three other South Africans (Tom van Vollenhoven, Alan Skene and Chris Landsberg), an Australian (Brian Bevan), two Scots (Brian Shillinglaw and Hugh Duffy), a Welshman (Danny Harris), and five English-born players. Vollenhoven, Skene, Bev Risman, Shillinglaw, Harris and Duffy were all former Rugby Union internationals for their respective countries. With both wing greats Bevan and Vollenhoven normally operating on the right flank in club games, Bevan had a rare outing on the left.

RUGBY LEAGUE XIII MASTERS

PLUCKY FIGHT BY NEW ZEALANDERS

Rugby League XIII 22 pts.,
New Zealanders 20

A FIGHTING come-back in the closing 20 minutes of an always interesting game at W h i t e City, Manchester, enabled the New Zealanders to shake the strong Rugby League XIII before going down to their sixth defeat of the tour.

Well beaten in the scrums, they had to fight for their chances, but the bunching of the forwards and faulty handling enabled the League to be masters for most of the game. Once they settled down the New Zealanders h t back with vigour and skill.

THE TEAMS

RUGBY LEAGUE XIII 22	NEW ZEALAND 20
(Colours — Red Jerseys and White Shorts)	(Colours — Black Jerseys with White "V's" and White Shorts)
1. F. GRIFFITHS (Wigan) — Captain Full Back	1. J. FAGAN Full Back
2. T. VAN VOLLENHOVEN (St. Helens) Right Wing	3. T. HADFIELD Right Wing
3. A. SKENE (Wakefield T.) Rt. Centre	9. R. BAILEY Rt. Centre
4. C. LANDSBERG (Leigh) Left Centre	10. R McCRACKEN/7 R. COOKE Left Centre
5. B. BEVAN (Warrington) Left Wing	4. B. REIDY Left Wing
6. B. RISMAN (Leigh) Stand-off	12. J. BOND Stand-off
7. B. SHILLINGLAW (Whitehaven) Scrum-Half	14. G. FARRAR Scrum-Half
8. A. THOMPSON (Swinton) Front Row	23. S. EDWARDS Front Row
9. L. McINTYRE (Oldham) Hooker	25. J. BUTTERFIELD Hooker
10. E. BATE (Widnes) Front Row	22. H. EMERY Front Row
11. D. HARRIS (Leigh) 2nd Row	18. D. HAMMOND — Captain 2nd Row
12. L. GILFEDDER (Warrington) 2nd Row	17. R. DUFFY 2nd Row
13. H. DUFFY (Salford) Loose Forward	16. B. CASTLE Loose Forward

Referee :	Touch Judges :
D. T. H. DAVIES (Manchester)	C. A. MOSELEY (Manchester) J. C. WHITFIELD (Manchester)

eleven

Old Trafford

Manchester United's Old Trafford stadium has firmly established itself as a modern 'Mecca' for Rugby League supporters, particularly for the Grand Final at the climax to the Super League season. It was officially opened in February 1910, with United – in the ascendancy having been League Champions in 1907/08 and FA Cup winners in 1909 – moving from Clayton, their base since 1893. In December 1920, 70,504 attended when Manchester United met Aston Villa in a League fixture, the ground record being set in 1939, when 76,962 watched the Grimsby Town-Wolverhampton Wanderers FA Cup semi-final.

The first time an oval ball appeared at the ground was in 1924 when Lancashire met the New Zealand Rugby Union tourists during October, the All Blacks winning 23-0 before 35,000 spectators. Rugby Union did not return until November 1997 when New Zealand beat England 25-8 – the first time in over a century that England had played in Manchester.

It was Rugby League neighbours, Salford, who first proposed taking a thirteen-a-side match to the ground in 1958. They had been due to entertain Leeds during October, but the match was postponed after Leeds qualified for the Yorkshire Cup final the same day. Salford, anxious not to lose revenue on one of their most attractive fixtures, approached United, who readily agreed to stage the match under floodlight on 5 November.

It was not until 1986/87 that Manchester United was approached again, this time by the Rugby League hierarchy. Old Trafford was hired for the First Test between Great Britain and Australia during October followed by the end-of-season Premiership final in May. Both paid off with record attendances for a Test (in Britain) and the Premiership final. Following that encouraging start, four further Test Matches have to date been taken to Old Trafford (including one against New Zealand), whilst the Premiership final and its successor, the Super League Grand Final, have been held at Old Trafford every season since.

During the 1989/90 season, two other prestige Rugby League events took place inside Old Trafford although, so far, it is the only occasion either has been held at the ground. The first, in October, saw British champions Widnes matched against their Australian counterparts, Canberra Raiders, in the World Club Challenge whilst in the second, during March, St Helens met Wigan in a Challenge Cup semi-final.

Two important Rugby League World Cup matches have also taken place at the ground. In 1995 – Rugby League's centenary year – thousands of Welsh men and women descended on Old Trafford to see Wales meet England in a semi-final, providing a colourful and unique experience for those present. Five years later, the final itself was played at Old Trafford as the irrepressible Australia defeated New Zealand in an all-Southern Hemisphere affair.